THE U

Skateboard
BOOK

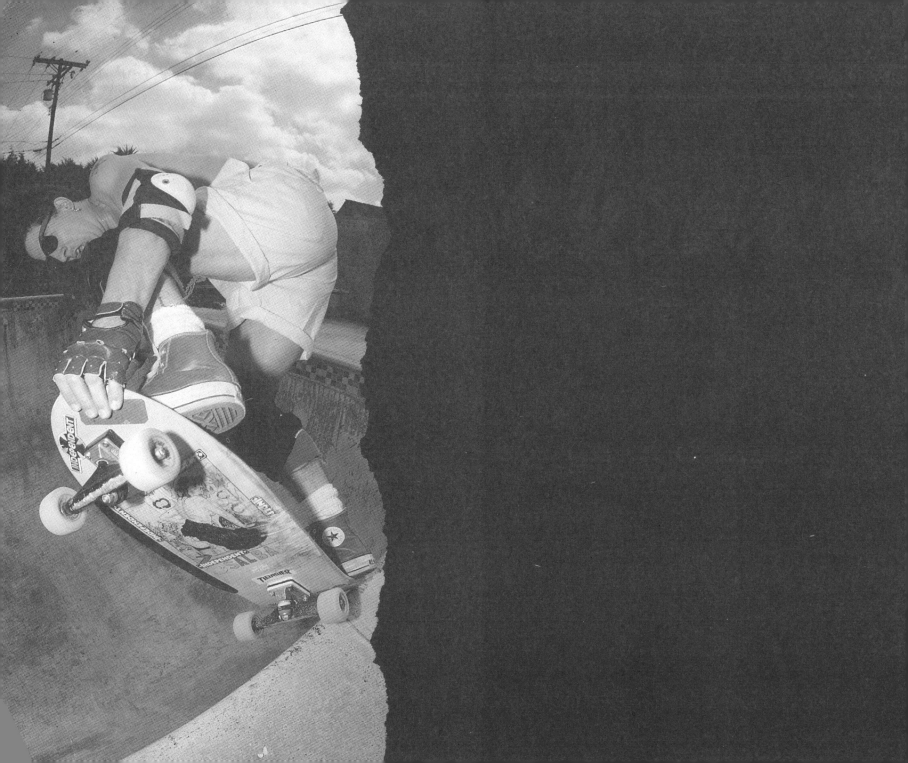

THE ULTIMATE

Skateboard

BOOK

by Albert Cassorla

Running Press • Philadelphia, Pennsylvania

Canadian representatives: General Publishing Co., Ltd., 30 Lesmill
Road, Don Mills, Ontario M3B 2T6.

International representatives: Worldwide Media Services, Inc.,
115 East Twenty-third Street, New York, NY 10010.

9 8 7 6 5 4 3 2 1
Digit on the right indicates the number of this printing.
Library of Congress Cataloging-in-Publication Number 88-42604.
ISBN 0-89471-564-X

Photographs: By Philip Bodor—p. 52 (upper left), p. 59 (right),
p. 63 (lower right), p. 64; © 1988 by Karen Brown—pp. 86-87;
© 1988 by Albert Cassorla—p. 5, p. 91 (right); © 1988 by Martha
Fried-Cassorla—p. 51, p. 128; © 1988 by Michael Funk, p. 41
(center); © 1988 by Richard Henkles—p. 58 (bottom), p. 65;
© 1988 by Keith Hershman—p. 9, p. 30, pp. 36-37, p. 41 (right), p. 52
(lower left), p. 57 (right), p. 66 (top), p. 73 (top right), p. 79 (lower
left), p. 91 (left), p. 95, p. 127; © 1987, 1988 by Steven Keenan—
p. 2, p. 4, p. 6 (left and right), p. 8, p. 17, p. 18 (right), p. 27 (right),
pp. 28-29, p. 38, p. 51 (center), p. 60 (left), p. 67 (left), p. 68 (lower
left), p. 70 (center), p. 72 (lower right) p. 74 (center and lower
right), p. 75 (lower right), p. 77, p. 79 (right), p. 88, p. 110, p. 120;
© 1987, 1988 by Richard Metiver—p. 31, p. 33, p. 40, p. 61, p. 90;
© 1988 by Aaron Sedway—p. 1, p. 7 (center), pp. 10-11, p. 24,
pp. 26-27, p. 39, p. 44 (left), pp. 45-48, p. 54 (center), p. 55 (left),
p. 58 (top), p. 66 (bottom), p. 69 (bottom), p. 80, p. 81 (left), p. 82
(upper left), p. 83 (lower left), pp. 94-95, p. 112, p. 114 (right),
p. 116 (right), p. 121; © 1988 by Steve Strommer—p. 50; © 1988
by Liz Vogdes—p. 49 (right); © 1987, 1988 by Mark
Zemnick—p. 7 (left and right), pp. 12-14, p. 18 (left), pp. 20-23,
p. 25, p. 35, p. 37 (right), pp. 42-43, p. 44 (right), p. 52 (right),
p. 53, p. 54 (right), p. 55 (right), p. 56, p. 57 (center), p. 59 (left),
p. 60 (right), p. 62, p. 63 (left, upper and center right), p. 67
(center and right), p. 68 (top left and right), p. 69 (top), p. 70 (left
and right), p. 71, p. 72 (upper and lower left), p. 73 (upper left
and bottom), p. 74 (left and upper right), p. 75 (left, center, and
upper right), p. 76, p. 78, p. 79 (upper left), p. 81 (center and
right), p. 82 (center), p. 83 (left and upper right), pp. 84-85, p. 87,
p. 89, p. 96, p. 99, p. 103, p. 107, p. 109, p. 113 (right), p. 114
(left), p. 115, p. 116 (left), p. 119, pp. 123-124.

The author would like to thank the following companies for
assistance with photographs: Airborne, Alva Skates, Gotcha
Sportswear, Hosoi Skates, Santa Cruz Skateboards; and
Vision Sports.

Additional photographs from *The Skateboarder's Bible* © 1976 by
Running Press—p. 6, p. 11 (right), pp. 15-16, p. 19, p. 32.

Cover design by Toby Schmidt
Cover photography © 1987, 1988 by Mark Zemnick (left—Christian
Hosoi; center—Mike Smith; right—Nicky Guerrero).
Back cover photography © 1988 by Richard Metiver (left—Corey
O'Brien) and © 1987 by Mark Zemnick (right—Nicky Guerrero).
Interior illustrations by Bruce Lohr
Graphics and symbols by Tony Vogdes and Liz Vogdes
Printed by Port City Press, Inc., Baltimore, MD.
Typography: ITC Cushing Book, Univers 49, Helvetica & Futura
by TypeMasters, Inc., West Conshohocken, PA. Choc by Letraset.

This book may be ordered by mail from the publisher. Please add
$1.50 for postage. *But try your bookstore first!*
Running Press Book Publishers
125 South Twenty-second Street
Philadelphia, Pennsylvania 19103

To Martha, Emma, and Benjamin,
who keep me rolling.

ACKNOWLEDGMENTS

Thanks...

...above all, to you—the skater and reader—for wanting to know more about this fantastic sport and for taking me along as your guide.

Also special thanks to the incredibly patient John Burke and Mark Kramer, who helped me translate countless twists and turns into instructions for skateboarding tricks; to Roger Brown, who extolled the virtues of freestyle trickery and dispensed some of its secrets; to Richard Roberts, owner of Spike's Skates in Philadelphia, who answered many questions while my computer took up his counter space; to Britt Parrott, for recounting his bird's eye view of the past ten years of skateboarding history; to Bruce Lohr, for his painstakingly accurate ramp illustrations; and to the people of Running Press, who have twice believed that this sport deserved its own book: publishers Lawrence and Stuart Teacher, and Cynthia Roberts, Liz Vogdes, Nancy Steele, and Elizabeth Zozom.

CONTENTS

PREFACE

Skateboarding is a wild, untamed thing—like the spirit of its riders. People invent skateboarding daily. People like you. And then they go out the next day and invent it again! That's the beauty of the sport, especially at this time in its history. Depending on when you want to start counting, skateboarding is more than 80 years old, but never has it been so free, so pure, and so multifaceted.

The Greek philosopher Heraclitus said, "You can never step into the same river twice." Ever flowing and changing, a river is always different. Only the name remains the same. Skateboarding, like a flowing river, is constantly evolving. The day it becomes a "how-to" process etched in stone is the day the sport will die. But that won't happen, because every skater develops in different ways, each adding a unique twist to the sport.

Twelve years ago I wrote a book called *The Skateboarder's Bible*. About 90 percent of what skaters do today was impossible back then. That's how far skateboarding has come. And it has a long way to go. Who knows what tricks will be invented next? Maybe 1440-degree airs. Or shredding the slanted faces of New York City skyscrapers.

But this book is for *now*—for making it easier to get from rollin' to rippin.' Instead of saying, "This is how it must be done," this book says, "Here's something you might try." 'Cause this is a free sport, except for the board. And skateboarding's gonna thrive as long as kids skate the streets of Tokyo, London, New York, San Francisco, Idaho Falls—practically any place that's paved.

Like the British Empire, the sun never sets on skateboarding. But *unlike* the British Empire, this one ain't gonna die.

Keep skating!

SKATEBOARDING

HISTORY

CHAPTER 1

Maybe you think skateboarding is a brand new sport. Maybe you think boards have always had kicktails, copers, tail domes, and really rad graphics. Maybe you think an alley oop backside air from a half-pipe is where skateboarding tricks began. Maybe you need a history lesson.

Skateboarding isn't something dreamed up in the past few years, when the sport was popping up across the United States and around the world. Skateboarding actually has a great history, with many interesting twists and turns.

Christian Hosoi launches
into a backside Japan air

No one person invented skateboarding. Nor did a committee. It came from the streets—the same place where skateboarding history is being made today. So how did this fantastic sport first get rolling? Here's the story, as I have been able to reconstruct it.

IN THE BEGINNING...

The forerunners of skateboards were rough-riding scooters made by nailing old-fashioned over-the-shoe roller skates onto two-by-fours. Most of these "scooter-boards" also had produce crates nailed onto the two-by-four, and projecting sticks attached to the top of the crate for handlebars. You pushed along with one foot and leaned left or right for whatever directional control you could get (not much).

Some of these scooters omitted the crate altogether. Skateboarding's scholars allege that this popular contraption, older than Grandpa's whiskers, was really the first skateboard. While some folks in California recall using scooterboards in the 1930s and 1940s, the earliest use anyone has claimed for them is in the summer of 1904.

This is somewhat beside the point. Those early devices, compared with today's custom boards, were merely planks on wheels. But there's no doubt that skateboarding's heritage lies in the harmonic convergence of these two juvenile pleasures: scooting and roller skating. Surfing was an important early influence, too, and many of the early skateboarders also were surfers.

THE 1950s: DAWN OF SKATEBOARDING

By the 1950s, roller skates featured smoother-riding clay wheels attached to double-action trucks—meaning the axles were no longer rigid, but could pivot and swivel from side to side, the way they do now. Some kids began attaching Union Hardware skates to planks by removing the rivets joining the skate to the shoe, and sawing through the metal strip that kept the trucks together. Smarter kids were removing the rubber cushions from these relatively stiff trucks to increase sideway movement and control.

Enter the Logan Brothers, who later became pro skateboarders and manufacturers. They recall riding on Roller Derby skates attached to plywood boards way back in 1958. In the same year, Bill Richards and his son Mark, both of Val Surf Shop in Dana Point, California, noticed a group that consistently attracted attention when they rode together. Bill and Mark recognized the similarity between surfing and skateboarding, as did many others, but they were the first to consider building boards for retail trade. They asked the Chicago Roller Skate Company to cut its double-trucked units in two and send Val Surf a shipment of the divided parts. These were mounted on square, wooden boards and sold for about $8. It was largely a basement operation—yet this was the genesis of skateboarding as a mass phenomenon.

Pools are for planting—and Eddie Elguera shows how with a sadplant

THE 1960s: SIDEWALK SURFIN'

Surfers were among the first to buy skateboards, which provided a pleasant diversion when there were no waves. The symbiotic relationship between skateboarding and surfing was apparent right from the start, and later grew to joint production and advertising in some companies.

Skateboarding has always fared best on the East and West coasts, with its popularity radiating inward to the Midwest. In the early days, surfers from California's San Fernando Valley first purchased the skateboards. Surfers who enjoyed the beaches at Malibu, Ventura, or Santa Monica also took to asphalt action on skateboards.

Skateboarding ollied out of the basement when the Patteson-Forbes Company began producing one of the first assembly line boards, but it was only a scooter-type model lacking flexible truck action, thus limiting control of the board. Still, the sport was picking up speed. By 1962, the hobby gained some recognition as "terra-surfing." One year later, skateboarding started to rip when Larry Stevenson—who some say *is* the Father of Skateboarding—started professional production of double-action boards shaped like surfboards. That had a lot of psycho-logical appeal to aficionados of "sidewalk surfing."

Stevenson's Makaha Company experimented with various materials in the early years, including plywood and foam, after the first Makaha board rolled off the production line in June 1963.

Within months, the nation's first skateboarding competition was held at Pier Avenue Junior High School in Hermosa, California. Contests there

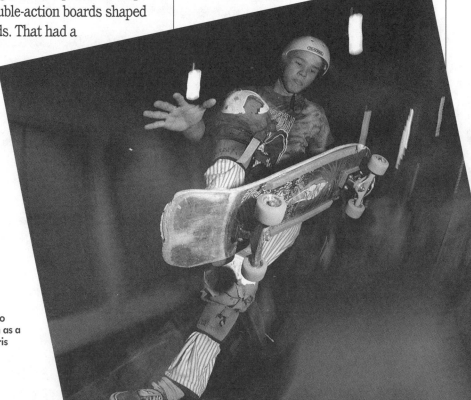

One-footed lien to tail, better known as a Madonna, by Chris Livingston

A top-quality '70s board, left, like this G&S model had a fiber glass and plywood deck; plastic toy store models, right, are making a comeback

and at Pacific Palisades High School drew some 100 spectators, a big number back then. Many of skateboarding's basic tricks originated in 1963, including nose and tail wheelies, handstands, headstands, 360s, high jumps (up to three feet), and slaloms.

The early contests did not emphasize downhill, and slaloms could not be held on a steep grade because of the poor turning capacity of those early boards. Nose wheelie spins were unknown. A popular contest event that now seems quaint was the "kick-turn race," in which the skater did a string of 180 turns from nose to tail all the way to the finish line.

The sport continued developing in the '60s as new manufacturers entered the fray: Hobie, Boss Man, Black Knight, and Super Surfer. You could buy a board for as little as $1.29 (!) or pay an astronomical $15 for a top-quality model. Motorized versions ran as much as $50. Companies like TriPac and Nash vied for

the business at the lower end of the price spectrum.

Skateboarding was now *red hot.* "The atmosphere was packaged insanity," recalls Steve Baseman, who worked for TriPac. "You couldn't make 'em fast enough." For three years, sales went straight up—Makaha's topped $4 million during that period and the small company was getting orders for as many as 20,000 boards a day.

Hobie came out with the first fiber glass board and also developed a truck especially for skateboarding. Though not a technical marvel by today's standards, it was fine for its time. Makaha marketed a melamine board—the T-C—that netted $250,000 in sales in a single day. Urethane wheels—which would later rev-

olutionize skateboarding—also made their debut in 1963. But the wheels were relatively expensive and manufacturers weren't willing to stick them on boards that typically retailed for $12.95.

Skateboarding garnered its status as a sport when Makaha fielded an exhibition team featuring Squeaky Blank, Danny Bearer, Larry Stevenson, and others. Then Vita-Pakt, a major orange juice manufacturer, made a splash in late 1963 by becoming a corporate sponsor for Hobie. No doubt, early thrashers drank O.J., but the real reason for Vita-Pakt's interest was that the company was owned by hotel magnate Conrad Hilton, whose sons persuaded their rich daddy to sink more than $2 million into Hobie. Flush with capital, Hobie offered the

Back in 1965, this Godzilla-sized ramp was used for competitions in Anaheim, California

Makaha team better terms—including free trips to Hawaii—and the whole team switched to Hobie. Small wonder.

The fad raged on. And it *was* a fad in most places, even as skateboarding was gaining recognition as a sport. To most kids, a skateboard was no different from a hula hoop or a Davy Crockett coonskin cap.

Interest began peaking in late 1964, when several contests were held at the Santa Monica Auditorium in California. About six months later, the First Annual National Skateboard Championships

were held at La Palma Stadium in Anaheim, California. The meet drew national press attention; all three networks covered the contest, which also was broadcast on ABC's "Wide World of Sports."

For those who attend today's national competitions, the event would seem tame. A twenty-foot-high ramp—considered gigantic in its time—was erected atop a metal-framed structure for the downhill run. But that height was considered too dangerous, even for experienced skaters, and it was lowered to

eleven feet. Concrete slabs were used for flatland slalom and trick areas. Winners were awarded $500 scholarships.

Now that skateboarding had arrived as a sport, its stars began turning pro and making a living. And since the establishment sports press wasn't completely covering skateboarding's rapid advance, *Skateboarder* magazine was born.

Skateboarder, edited by John Severson, ripped along for four issues until the mag temporarily went under in October 1965. And mainstream media didn't miss the craze entirely. *Life* and *Newsweek* magazines both did features on skateboarding in May 1965. *Skater Dater*, a short film with a slightly sweet plot, charmed national audiences with scenes of skateboarders in action.

Meanwhile, skateboard sales started to soar. An estimated 50 million boards were made during skateboarding's first incarnation. Looking back, the sport's popularity in the 1960s is truly amazing when you consider the equipment was so inferior that the wheels couldn't roll over anything bigger than a cigarette butt without dumping the rider. And that's what eventually caused skateboarding's first downfall. Skaters rode those treacherous boards into all kinds of accidents.

1965: Skateboarding Bails

In what seemed like seconds after its arrival as a sport, skateboarding was booted out the back door as a menace to society. "Too Much Moxie Breeds Mayhem in the Streets," shouted *Life*. *Good Housekeeping* hit the deck with this pithy observation: "Seldom has a sport fad produced as many fractured arms, wrists, and legs, concussions, and lacerations as skateboarding." Next to nuclear war, skateboarding seemed to be the thing that worried parents most.

Doctors agreed. The California Medical Association called boards "a new medical menace," a phrase that frequently would be repeated in the weeks ahead. In Los Angeles, twenty-five skateboarders a month were getting hurt–two-thirds of them breaking bones. In New Rochelle, New York, fifty skaters a month were being hospitalized after skateboarding accidents, half of them with broken bones.

The American Medical Association joined the denunciation orgy. Dr. John C. Wilson, then vice chairman of the AMA's orthopedic surgery division, told *Good Housekeeping* that with the advent of skateboarding, "I have had the occasion to observe fractures about the elbow of a magnitude previously not seen in growing bone."

A major car insurance company released this special alert about skateboarding: "We strongly urge that during the forthcoming spring and summer driv-

Mean lien to tail by Erik Castro

ing season that you keep an especially sharp alert for this new traffic menace." By August 1965, doomsday was in sight as the National Safety Council issued a warning about skateboarding safety.

Twenty cities banned the sport from sidewalks and streets in what *Newsweek* termed "adult backlash" as town after town reacted. Skateboards were confiscated. Police officials in some cities approached department stores and asked that skateboards be removed from the shelves as a public service. In Portland, Oregon–then the only American city to set aside a road for skateboarders–the cops became vigilant. They even apprehended a skateboarding dog named

Part of today's repertoire is the tuck-knee invert–as Joe Johnson demonstrates

Tiger. Since it wasn't illegal for dogs to skateboard, authorities booked the magnificent skate-pooch on a leash law violation.

Tiger's detainment was the only light moment in a pretty bleak period. In the words of veteran Steve Baseman, "Legislation was passed. Then one Sunday, the craze died as quickly as it had started."

"I can just about call it to the week, if not the day," adds Makaha founder Larry Stevenson. "It was mid-November 1965 when things just died. One week I was getting so many orders, people were leaving them on my doorstep just so I'd see them when I left for work in the morning. The next week, I was getting $75,000 in cancellations in a single day!"

Not everyone agrees that unsafe conditions brought about skateboarding's first demise. One who saw flaws in the sport was veteran skater Brian Logan. "It got boring," Logan recalls. "The wheels just didn't give you enough to do. There was no full-on slalom and just not enough variety to keep the thing going."

By the beginning of 1966, skateboarding was dead as a national pastime. The next eight years were dry, even though a few diehards in the San Fernando Valley

Micke Alba knows pipes are part of a skater's terrain

clung to the sport. Larry Stevenson, who lost $250,000 in 1966, tried to revive skateboarding in 1969–and promptly blew another $40,000.

Then Makaha formed a new team to renew enthusiasm and got Bruce and Brad Logan, Ty Page, Rusty Johnson, and a few others to stage exhibitions. Fifty thousand boards were sold, and the sport was slowly on the upswing.

THE 1970s: SKATEBOARDING REBOUNDS

Skateboarding owes its 1970s renaissance almost entirely to to one man–Frank Nasworthy. His indispensible contribution? Introducing the polyurethane wheel in 1973. Many skaters wrongly believe that Nasworthy *invented* the wheel–that is, the polyurethane wheel. Actually, he was the first to effectively market it and to develop a wheel specifically for skateboards.

Nasworthy's tale begins in 1970, when he spent some time at Creative Urethanes, Inc., a plastics factory in Purcelville, Virginia, that made a small number of urethane wheels to be sold at roller rinks. Although serious roller skaters found them slow, beginners liked their greater traction.

One day, an employee of Creative Urethanes was discarding a batch of the wheels when Nasworthy asked if he could have some. "Sure," he was told, "take as many as you like." Seeing the possibilities, he bought 1,000 wheels on credit and moved to California. Working as a waiter, he planned to peddle the wheels in his off-hours.

Although he showed them at every surf shop in San Diego, he couldn't find any takers. Nasworthy eventually convinced a couple of shops in Southern California to stock his wheels–and they were a solid success with skateboarders. The wheels vastly improved maneuverability, which encouraged skaters to take their boards out more often. Enthusiasm began to simmer, so Nasworthy took $700 saved from his restaurant job and started the Cadillac Wheels Company. He made his own mold, specified his own mix of urethane ingredients, and got Creative Urethanes to put "Cadillac" in block letters on the side of the wheel.

Nasworthy bought a half-page ad in *Surfer Magazine* and started a trend in wheel advertising that continues to this day. By 1974, he had sold 120,000 wheels –more than Creative Urethanes had sold

Urethane wheels put new spirit into the sport of skateboarding in the 1970s

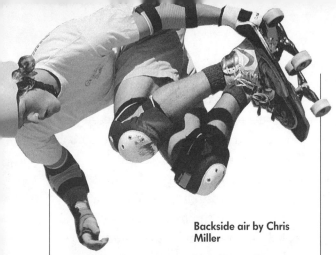

Backside air by Chris Miller

to roller skaters in seven years. With no patent, contract, or financial backing, Nasworthy almost singlehandedly promoted the product that was synonymous with the rebirth of skateboarding. For this, we all owe him credit.

By 1974, skateboarding was rolling again in California, and the East Coast caught on in 1975. Surfer Publications, which published *Skateboarder* in the 1960s, revived the magazine. Issues became more and more popular until they sold out virtually as soon as they hit the stands.

Skateboard manufacturers went back into production. New firms opened up and surfboard makers added skateboards to their lines. Competitions became a hot way to promote the sport. South Bay's X-Caliber division sponsored one such event, drawing 125 skaters to

Torrance, California, in July 1975. Two months later, some 6,500 fans turned out in Del Mar, California, for the World Pro-Am Contest.

Slalom and speed racing were hot then, and big ramps meant more speed. One such example was the loveable monster built for the World Pro-Am—a gargantuan Bahne ramp that was 120 feet long, 24 feet wide, and 12 feet high. This dinosaur was shipped around California for numerous events; reconstruction took twelve skilled carpenters eight hours to complete.

Skateboarding sailed through the next few years. The boards got a bit longer and wider, which made pool riding popular. Skateparks—Gunite-coated wonderlands—opened around the country, mostly because municipalities still discouraged street skating.

By 1979, with the sport largely dependent on skateparks, skateboarding bailed again. Many skateparks were poorly built and began to have insurance liability problems. In that one year, some 75 to 80 percent of skateparks closed their doors *and* the National Safety Council issued a highly critical report of skateboarding.

Kick the sky with a judo lien air—Christian Hosoi-style

THE *1980*s & BEYOND: STATE OF THE ART SKATEBOARDING

The resurgence of skateboarding in the late '70s produced many technical advances: decks were about 10″ wide and 30″ long, just as they are now; steep kicktails were designed; the edges of wheels were rounded and becoming conical. In short, you had state-of-the-art boards—but you also had a dying sport.

By 1980, most of the parks had closed and skaters simply quit despite the exciting evolution in skateboard design. As in the past, however, a few staunch thrashers refused to turn in their boards.

So the sport continued to develop technically even though it wasn't that popular nationally. Perhaps because they lacked attention, skateboarding's diehards had time to hone their craft. This could be why skaters who were active in the early '80s—Steve Caballero, Mike Smith, Neil Blender, Billy Ruff—maintained their status for years. Even so, they were unable to support themselves as skate pros in this "skateboarding depression."

Many of those who stuck with skateboarding decided to do something for themselves in the early '80s: build bigger ramps. The big ramps of the late '70s were U-shaped. By 1981, the flat stretches between the transitions started getting longer. The width was 8 to 16 feet —bigger than before, but small by today's standards. One forerunner of the really big ramps was built at the Ramp Ranch in Atlanta in 1983—32 feet wide and 40 feet long!

Bigger, better ramps naturally set the stage for bigger, better tricks. Although smalls airs were spotted back in the late '70s, airs were hitting a range of three to four feet by 1983. Handplants, rock-n-rolls, and frontside grinds grew popular.

Skateboarding in the early '80s got a boost from formation of the National Skateboard Association through a Boy Scouts' Explorer Post in San Diego. In 1981, the NSA offered $4,000 in prize money at The Rusty Harris Series, a contest held in the memory of a skater and skateboarding photographer who died of leukemia. Everyone active in skateboarding agrees that the NSA has made an enormous contribution to the rising interest in skateboarding. Since 1982, it has held organized contests annually for amateur and professional skateboarders and roller skaters.

Others had faith that skateboarding would survive. Edward J. Riggins founded *Thrasher* magazine in the inauspicious year of 1981. Edited by Kevin Thatcher, a longtime skateboarder, *Thrasher* gave board manufacturers who were still in the field a place to advertise, and it offered a communication forum for skaters.

By 1983, interest was definitely on the rise. The first big pro ramp contest–The Great Desert Ramp Battle–was held in Palmdale, California. Back East,

Transitions are great for Cody Boat's layback slide

the Mid-Eastern Skateboard Series (MESS) helped re-ignite the sport. MESS was a kind of touring contest involving five different ramps in Ohio and Virginia. Participants included Britt Parrott of Nashville, Bryan Ridgeway of Huntington, West Virginia, and Marty Jimenez of Cincinnati. About 50 skaters participated, but crowd turnout was low and there were no cash prizes.

California had all the pro contests, even though cash prizes were typically no more than $500. The hot places to skate were Upland Skatepark (the Pipeline) and Del Mar Skatepark in Del Mar, California. Interest in the sport now centered in San Francisco and extended as far south as San Diego. On the East Coast, skaters created a mecca at Kona Skateboard Park in Jacksonville, Florida.

In California, the Midwest, and elsewhere, little skateboardng magazines began to flourish. These "skate rags" nurtured a kind of network by including names and addresses of skaters. In 1982, there was only one such publication; two years later there were 75 "zines" nationwide. They told mainly what was happening locally, with photos of skaters or contests.

Skateboarding puts focus on personal performance, as Bill Tocco's invert demonstrates

Transworld Skateboarding, one of two mass circulation skateboarding magazines, was founded in 1983 by Larry Balma and Peggy Cozens. Begun with just 40 pages, the magazine doubled its pages and distribution within two years. By 1987, circulation stood at 215,000.

The MESS was held again in 1984, but many of the best shredders who had skated a year earlier followed the action to California and turned pro. In Del Mar, there were new ramp and "street style" competitions. People took over parking lots and streets for contests. Ollies, which had been popular on ramp as far back as the 1970s, became a big part of the street skating scene by 1985.

Skateparks were now completely eclipsed by street skating. Skateboarding in the '80s put more focus on doing things for yourself—rather than relying on skateparks. The sport's new growth enabled companies like Vision Skateboards to open shop and grow by leaps and bounds. Today, Vision, Santa Cruz, and Powell-Peralta dominate the field. Tomorrow, who knows?

In Europe, skateboarding followed about a year behind the United States. European championships also started in the early '80s; Sweden, England, France, and Germany became the biggest centers of interest.

Back across the Atlantic, newer tricks played a big part in ramp competitions. Many serious skaters were pushing lip trickery—moves at the edge of the ramp—instead of high-flying aerials. They felt that aerials are easier than some less spectacular tricks that deserve more regard. But there's something to be said for flash. Mike McGill invented the McTwist in the 1984 Swedish Summer Camp and brought it public that autumn back in Del Mar. Then Tony Hawk, who already was drawing attention with his 360 airs and risky ramp tricks, perfected the McTwist in late '85 and 1986. These fantastic tricks drew a great deal of interest and helped to truly create skateboarding's third incarnation.

During a tail stall, Bill Danforth takes a second to reflect

By 1985, broadcasting and film started picking up on the sport. Commercials and parts of movies began featuring the new, funkier skateboarding.

Response to a skateboarding contest at Canada's Expo '86 confirmed skateboarding's upward swing. The Transworld Skateboard Championships held in Vancouver that August drew participants from the United States, Canada, United Kingdom, Australia, France, Italy, Germany, Czechoslovakia, Brazil, and Sweden. The crowds grew, too. Bigger contests began drawing upwards of 5,000 spectators.

By 1986, skateboard sales doubled. Total sales ran to 450 million items, including wheels, decks, and accessories. The NSA also found 1986 a good time to break away from the Boy Scouts and seek its own non-profit status. The following year, the NSA was running two major programs—an International Pro-Tour and a National Amateur Program—on a $300,000 budget, including $100,000 in prize money.

Boned frontside air by Jason Urbisci

Even Hollywood was impressed. A minor skateboarding movie, *Thrashin'*, came out in 1986. For most skaters, the action shots were a bore—it was a "guy gets girl" love story. But on the video front, manufacturer Powell-Peralta released the more cinematically interesting and revealing "The Search for Animal Chin" in 1987. The third in a series of videos sponsored by Powell-Peralta, Animal Chin featured an enormous W-shaped double-ramp with a flat trough. The shooting, editing, and cutting of Animal Chin—especially in the ramp sequences—established a new standard for skating on film. Parts of it appeared in an MTV special and it was one of the first videos to penetrate the general market.

Skateboard sales continued to grow through 1987, hitting an estimated $500 million industry-wide. And the sport's image continued to be sullied by concerns about safety. Some 35,000 kids under 15 took a trip to the emergency room in 1985 because of skateboarding accidents; in 1986, the figure swelled to 58,000, according to the Consumer Product Safety Commission.

Skateboarding in the 1980s spawned a number of new sports—like snowboarding. These boards, popular at ski resorts —or on any snow-covered hill—let skateboarders perform many of the same exciting maneuvers on six inches of powder. There's even fingerboarding—practicing tricks with a tiny skateboard that's easy to hide from your teacher! And summer skateboarding camps are springing up to help skaters improve their moves and polish their style. Even the pros like camps such as the one in Bourges, France, that draws the world's top skaters during the summer.

Today, there are as many as 1.5 million skateboarders nationwide and another one million around the world. Pro skateboarders can earn $75,000 to $150,000 a year. Most of the dough comes from equipment endorsements, with contest prize money providing extra gravy.

Kevin Staab, right, and Tony Magnusson oblige fans with their autographs

By 1986, the pro contest schedule was so intense that the sport lost a lot of its spontaneity. Runs became very predictable because so many contests were held too close together. But manufacturers and others in the industry decided to resolve the problem by spreading out the contests.

Streetstyle contests have grown more popular. Though not as dramatic as ramp contests, they're perhaps closer to the spirit of skating. Skateboarding has truly become a people's sport, open to anyone with a board and a strong desire to skate.

In the next few years, we may see an expansion of skateboarding jams—sessions where skaters do their own thing while grooving on live or recorded music. In that kind of a non-competitive atmosphere, people are free to take chances and do what they feel—instead of what'll please the judges or thrill the crowds.

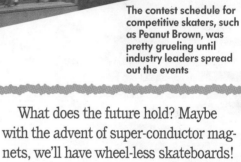

The contest schedule for competitive skaters, such as Peanut Brown, was pretty grueling until industry leaders spread out the events

What does the future hold? Maybe with the advent of super-conductor magnets, we'll have wheel-less skateboards! Imagine gliding along on a thin cushion of air into the horizon. Nobody knows if we'll reach the era of super-conducting skateboards. But one thing's for sure—we'll always be riding, and for the same reason people have been rippin' since 1904:

A skateboard is an implement of pleasure.

EQUIPMENT & MAINTENANCE

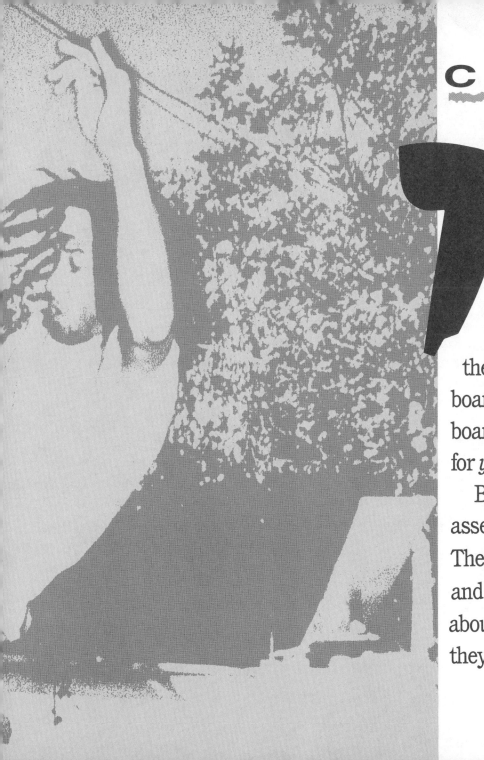

CHAPTER 2

he best skaters around the world build their own boards. They select decks, trucks, and wheels to suit their style and terrain. Some like a basic board. Others customize with copers, nose bones, tail domes, and lappers. Copy the pros and you'll have the best rippin' rad board around, right? No way. What makes a board first-rate is the fact that it works well for *you*.

Boards for beginners usually are pre-assembled and ready to roll. These are basically toys, and the best you can say about most of them is that they'll let you learn the fundamentals. Heavy-duty skaters usually look down on prefab models. Once you're hooked on building a quality board, it's sort of like buying a stereo system—you know what you want, and you select components to suit your tastes and needs.

If you're the parent of an 11-year-old and footing the bill for your kid's board, consider the skater and his skill level. Is

Smooth copings limit wear on John Gibson's board

your child big? Fat? (Be honest!) Small? Is he into street skating (up, over, or around sidewalk obstacles) or freestyle flips and other tricks? Does he want a big board? Smaller boards—29" or shorter—are quickly gaining popularity and are better suited to smaller riders.

Look for three basic qualities in your skateboard:
1. Light weight
2. Strength
3. Responsiveness

Even if you buy a complete, ready-to-roll board, you're still looking for these characteristics. But before you lay out your hard-earned cash, shop around. Try out a friend's board. See if you like the way it rides, the way the trucks snap back, the length, and the cut. Just remember that your pal Radical Randy's board won't ride exactly like yours—you'll be fine tuning, adding riser pads, copers, and so on until the board is an extension, an expression, of you.

You can build a board to suit your needs—esthetically and athletically—at a local skate shop or, if you know your boards well, through the mail. In any case, let's start with where you put your feet...

DECKS

Almost all decks are seven-ply Canadian maple, although manufacturers are constantly developing new materials or testing new ways to use traditional materials. However, engineering studies have shown that plywood offers the best properties, so your basic board remains seven-ply maple. You'll find it's the industry standard for pro boards.

You may have heard of "Boneite," a synthetic sort of sophisticated plywood developed by skateboard manufacturer Powell-Peralta in response to the tremendous shortage of rock-hard maple. Early designs included two plies of poplar, which weakened the board, but the newer XT Boneite has gone exclusively with maple ply. This is a little heavier than the earlier Boneite and most boards on the market.

G & S still uses fiber glass, a deck that was popular in the late 1960s but no longer the board of choice for many skaters. Aluminum boards also are available, but not widely used.

Next consider shape and length–both matters of taste and use. Your basic board for vertical riding is 10″ wide and 30″ long. Depending on your preference, look for a hammerhead or a notched nose, which has cuts near the nose to facilitate grabs. However, these bigger boards are losing popularity as skateparks close and pool riding dies down.

Today's basic board features a kicktail with an angle of about 30 degrees. This design improvement was developed in the 1970s and enables today's skaters to pivot, compress and jump, and use the back wheels as a fulcrum. A kicktail is crucial to most tricks, including spins and ollies. Try the Alva TriTail, with an extremely steep tail and a very concave deck, for really great ollies. Brand X also has a similar Diamond Tail model.

Mini-boards–9¾″ × 29½″–are built for street use, which is where most of the action is across America and around the world. The Alva mini Punk Smith and the Caballero are popular lines. The deeper your side cuts, the lighter the board and the better for skating street since you're less concerned about having a place to land on the board. Side cuts also help you grab.

If you're into freestyle, get a 7″ × 27″ board. The kicktail has only a slight angle; in fact, the front and the back are almost identical. This helps when bouncing pogos (on the end of a vertical board) because you wouldn't want to bounce on a standard kicktail since it would hit the ground at a sharp angle.

No matter what kind of deck you choose, be sure to cover it with grip tape. Don't be a poseur and worry about your graphics showing–cover your deck and skate safe. Check out Madrid's "fly-paper," a lighter grip tape that's super-grippy.

Graphics belong under boards–reserve the topside for grip tape

Axle grinds are tough on equipment, so buy a board built to last

TRUCKS

Put simply, trucks are used to attach the wheels to the deck. But it's *not* that simple. They put action, maneuverability, and versatility into your ride. The truck holds your axles, bearings, and wheels, and allows them to pivot, and you to turn. Sophisticated skaters know their trucks and put a lot of emphasis on getting trucks that work well for them.

Trucks are mostly aluminum, except for the axles, which are made of steel. Some trucks are magnesium; very expensive, but light. Tracker makes an Ultralight with a plastic baseplate that's popular because of the weight savings.

When you're buying a truck, you want it to be light and strong. And you want it to fit the deck! On some 10″ boards, for instance, a 149 mm truck may be too small. Anything smaller is definitely undersized. Judge what's right by making sure that when you turn, the edge of the wheel should come to or just beyond the edge of the board.

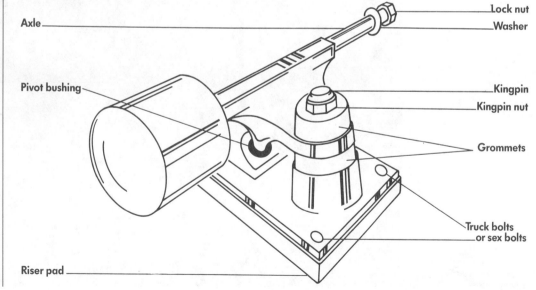

Axle

Pivot bushing

Riser pad

Lock nut

Washer

Kingpin

Kingpin nut

Grommets

Truck bolts or sex bolts

The most popular trucks are 159 or 169 mm. The 169s are good for tall skaters (over six feet) and for pool or ramp. The 159s are good for street or mini-boards. Thunder, Venture, and Gullwing make popular standard trucks. Tracker and Indy produce the only freestyle trucks—101 mm wide—which keep your wheels flush with the side of the board. Generally, freestyle trucks are a little tighter than streetstyle.

Grommets are thick urethane washers that help control truck action and they vary in durability; a hard grommet gives you tighter action, a softer one offers more play.

Riser pads are cushions between the truck and the board. They act as secondary shock absorbers and come in two sizes: half-inch and quarter-inch. Quarter-inch riser pads are lighter but offer less comfort; half-inch pads give more cushion and are better for beginners.

By the way, always keep a skate key or elephant wrench handy. When you buy your trucks, they'll probably be too loose and you'll need to adjust them.

Trucks do get loose, so pay special attention to securing yours well. Use high-quality nuts and screws to attach your hardware. Some state-of-the-art hardware—like Powell-Peralta's Thunderbolts—requires only a hammer and nut driver or socket wrench to attach your trucks. You'll find this to be more expensive than other hardware, but also reuseable. Be sure to get the right bolt size: 1½″ or 1¼″, depending on the thickness of your riser pad.

Most hardware comes with a Ny-lock built-in washer. Some manufacturers provide washers to add when you attach your hardware.

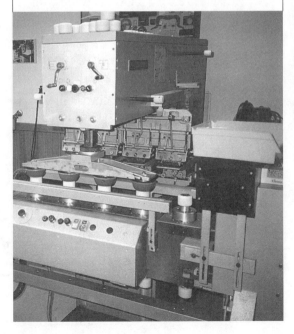

WHEELS

Wheels are where it all happens. Just as the invention of the wheel saved civilization from the Stone Age, refinement of

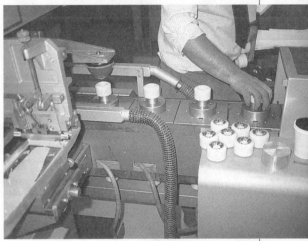

Before machines like these made urethane wheels, skaters rolled on hard clay and steel— a rough ride, enough to rattle your brain

the wheel rescued skateboarding from extinction in the 1970s. The introduction of polyurethane wheels vastly improved board control and today's skaters won't stand—or roll—for anything less.

But there's also variety in the wheels you choose. They come in various hardnesses, each appropriate for a different use although no type is mandatory for any situation. You'll find Santa Cruz, Gordon and Smith, Alva, Powell-Peralta, and Vision make the most popular brands. Here are some guidelines to help you choose:

Durometer	Use
78, 80, 85–Soft	Beginning street
90, 92, 95–Medium	Regular street
97, 98–Hard	Pool and ramp

Most wheels are 60 mm in diameter, although 57 mm and 58 mm are gaining popularity. Larger wheels offer more wheel surface and better balance. Experienced skaters prefer smaller wheels, which are lighter and faster. But some big wheels—68 mm, for example—are extremely narrow and very fast. Dyed wheels tend to have more oxides and are slightly slower due to friction with the road or ramp.

Wheel bearings, which allow the wheel to turn, are a key factor in outfitting your board. But not all bearings are created equal. There are three types, and it pays to know about them before investing in a new set of wheels. If you're ordering by mail, make sure you know what you are getting. The types are:

Loose Bearings—Avoid them completely. They get filthy, loose, and offer no consistency. They're common on toy-type boards.

Single-shielded Bearings—These are poured into a case but covered only on one side, so dirt still gets in and the bearings can pop out. Skip these, too.

Double-shielded or Full-precision Bearings—The best kind. These are lubricated internally and never fall out. Since they're encased, they're also faster. Major brands include GMN from Germany, NMB from Italy, and Powell Swiss bearings.

If you have loose or single-shielded bearings, maintenance is especially important. Don't ignore your bearing spacers, those important little pieces of metal between the bearings in each wheel. They keep the turn of the wheel consistent, and actually help you ride faster.

Skating in the rain kills your bearings —even double-shielded ones can rust almost overnight. Ripping through a puddle can ruin a laminated board. So if it's raining, walk and carry your board. Heading out into a downpour? Put your board in a plastic bag.

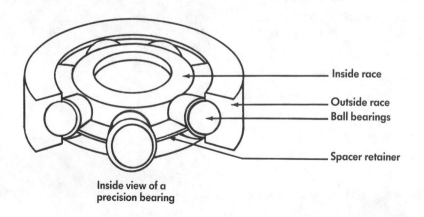

Inside view of a precision bearing

Inside race
Outside race
Ball bearings
Spacer retainer

SETTING UP YOUR BOARD

Most decks come pre-drilled for the trucks, but you may want to move your trucks back to make more nose for grabbing. When doing this, be very, very careful to align them properly. If you align your front truck slightly differently from your back truck, you won't be able to skate straight. Use a carpenter's right angle to mark your drilling X's exactly below the manufacturer's original holes.

Attaching wheels is pretty easy. First remove the axle nut and any washers. Assuming your bearings and spacers are in the wheel, put a washer on; then the wheel; now a second washer; and finally the axle nut. Tighten hard, and then loosen one quarter-turn.

Remember that not all wheels are reversible! Your best clue is that the graphics usually are printed on the outside.

Monty Nolder, left, and Christian Hosoi in the Santa Cruz/Speed Wheels office

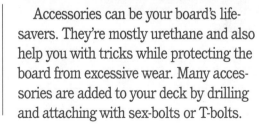

ACCESSORIES

Accessories can be your board's lifesavers. They're mostly urethane and also help you with tricks while protecting the board from excessive wear. Many accessories are added to your deck by drilling and attaching with sex-bolts or T-bolts.

Try to avoid wood screws, which chew up the deck. Bolts add only a few dollars to the cost, but they're definitely worth it.

Rails are your most important accessory, and essential for rail slides. They're like below-board handles when you're grabbing in the air. Some skaters like them close to the edge; others put them 2″ from the edge. It's a matter of where you're accustomed to grabbing.

Longer rails make rail slides easier. Make sure your rail starts at the back of your front wheels and goes all the way back. Don't put them close to where the actual wheels move. Esthetically, rails also protect your graphics—dear to the heart of many a skater.

(Speaking of graphics, go for what turns you on—stickers, war paint, whatever. Your board's look is entirely personal. Accept no instructions, even from books about skateboards.)

Short ribs or short rails are placed on either side of the tail bone. These cover the space between the tail and the rear wheels.

Nose bones, tail bones, tail skids, or tail domes are attachments that protect the underside of the board. Urethane is faster than plywood and also makes for easier slides. Always put the female T-bolt or sex-bolt through the top of the deck, and the male through the bottom.

Lappers are plastic devices to attach near the back truck where you curb hop; they protect your back truck kingpin from getting trashed on curbs. Copers protect the underside of the truck hanger, which houses the axle.

THE MAINTENANCE CHECK

After you've bought the board to suit your needs, protect your investment (and your health!) with regular maintenance. *Every time* you skate, make sure your board is in good shape. Think of your skateboard as a machine. You wouldn't take off in a jet plane that wasn't maintained, would you? So why risk airs on a board that's ignored? Here are some maintenance tips to make your board last:

1. Check your deck for cracks, dirt, or loose grip tape. When your deck is badly cracked, don't risk life and limb—replace it.
2. Spin all four wheels before each outing. You may find you have a slow wheel, caused by a rusty bearing or dirt.
3. Twist each of your four axle lock-nuts to assure tightness.
4. Check the action on your kingpin to make sure it's the way you want it. The one thing you don't want is a surprise.
5. Be sure your truck bolts are tight.
6. Keep grip tape in good shape. Coating your full board is wisest.

Along with these basics, there are some other important safeguards you can take. For example, if you do a lot of tail slides, it's smart to frequently replace your skid plate or tail slide. It's cheaper than replacing the board.

Use nose bones or guards to protect your deck; lappers and copers for your trucks. Lappers are particularly helpful when gliding up curbs, since they cut the pavement's resistance. They also help you avoid getting hung up at the lip, or coping, on a ramp.

Unlike your body, every part of a truck is replaceable. Most skate shops carry replacement parts. Parts you might want to replace from time to time include:

- baseplate
- hanger
- pivot bushing
- kingpin/kingpin nut
- washers
- truck bolts
- riser pads

Try to stick with the same manufacturer when choosing replacement parts. Baseplates, which join the truck mechanism to the board, tend to crack on one of the four corners, or they split in half. Hangers crack or get ground down beyond recognition. Truck and pivot bushings, which prevent erosion in the baseplate, get split and squeezed out. Kingpins control the flexibility of your truck action. Kingpins may split and kingpin nuts get stripped; if so, you'll find your trucks loosening much more

quickly than expected. Washers break or get bent up around the kingpin nut. Plastic riser pads tend to crack; urethane risers will last the life of a board.

To replace any of these, just take your truck apart. It's a pretty simple matter and takes only a couple of minutes. Remove the kingpin nut and slide everything off.

Take time to regularly examine your trucks, and don't overlook your mounting bolts. The truck bolts (or Powell-Peralta sex bolts) should always be tight against the baseplate.

Watch your wheels, too. Replace wheels that become beveled on one side and no longer make contact. Power slides and other tricks wear out your wheels fast.

Pros such as Christian Hosoi know the value of keeping a board in top condition for safe skating

Remember that your board has to suit you, and no one else. Not your pool-riding pal, not the local ramp pro, not your Dad or Mom. You're the one who's thrashin'—not them. Build or buy a board that feels good and rides well for you. Once you've acquired that special board, take care of it—and it'll take care of you.

SAFETY, ATTITUDE, STYLE

CHAPTER 3

Skateboarding is progressing so fast that yesterday's dangerous tricks quickly become safe—or they *seem* safe compared to the newer, riskier tricks. Tricks are concocted continually, many of them by star skaters who may be light years ahead of other thrashers—including you.

So what's really safe? After all, "safe" for someone else may be elementary action for you. No real rules apply, but here are six guidelines to keep a skater's body and soul in one piece:

THE SKATEBOARD SAFETY SIX

1. Develop a safety-conscious attitude.
2. Expect to progress in stages—not by leaps and bounds.
3. Wear the right protective gear for each situation.
4. Don't wind through traffic. A skateboard is a means of transportation, but it's no match for a city bus.
5. Don't skate when or where you have a good chance of wiping out.
6. Do a regular maintenance check before each outing, and as necessary (see page 34).

Frontside pipe thruster by
Steve Alba

The toughest part at the beginning is deciding what's safe for you. Start with the basics: kick-turns, slides, grinds. (See Chapter 5 on tricks.) As you progress, your balance will improve quickly and more difficult tricks will come naturally, and safely. You'll be doing airs and ollies before you know it, so don't push yourself at the start and *don't* cave in to peer pressure. Just because Shreddin' Sammy can ollie flip the front steps at school, should you do the same? Heck no! Don't forget that your parents will put an end to your glorious skating career faster than you can say "tuck-knee eggplant" if you mess up your legs during your first week on a board!

The biggest mistake beginning skaters make is trying to do too much too soon. Once you get the basics down, it's much easier to finesse the harder tricks. You know the expression, "You have to crawl before you can walk"? In skateboarding, it's translated as: "Ya gotta slappy grind before you can rail slide on hand railings."

Start with "street" skating in empty parking lots or on sidewalks. Skating on ramps requires more experience with board control, which you'll pick up while developing your street style.

Once you move on to ramp tricks, begin with grinds, rock-n-rolls, or axle stalls. Then progress to inverts, method airs, or other tougher maneuvers you see in the magazines.

When skating ramp, *always, always, always* wear knee pads. You'll bail as surely as it rains in Oregon. Anyway, you don't want your kneecap ripped off by a nail. It's very unpleasant.

Wear helmets, elbow pads, wrist guards, gloves, or other protective gear for intense sessions. Helmets shield you from more than the ramp itself. There's a lotta stuff coming—like coping, your board, and other skaters "dropping in."

Hi-top sneakers are necessary to keep your feet in good shape, especially your ankles, which are easy to tweak. Look for sneaks with reinforcement on the side because that's where they tend to tear when you ollie.

Smart, experienced skaters wear the right gear. And a few experienced skaters—if the truth be told—sometimes skate around traffic. But they won't take unnecessary risks to get where they're going. In the beginning, don't even go near traffic. Stick to sidewalks, which aren't really kid stuff; most have more interesting obstacles than you'll find on the street.

Night skating can be fun. You can session benches and obstacles without hassle. There's no one to throw you out of cool spots because they're all asleep! Just remember drivers will have trouble seeing you at night, so stay on the sidewalk.

Use your brain when you scout the terrain. Gravel, dirt, and sand are not skater-friendly–this goes for both your board and your body. We've already talked about the damage that rain can wreak on your bearings. The same goes for snow. If there's snow on the ground and you just gotta skate, find a piece of pavement that's been cleared.

Skate rad with the right safety gear–John Gibson does

39

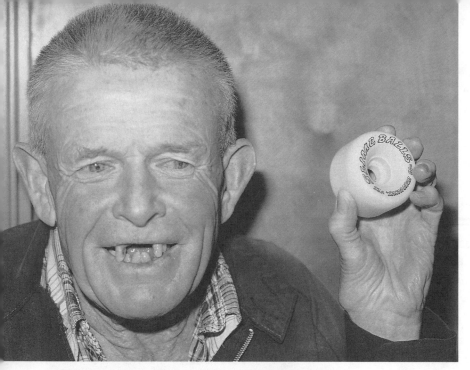

J. Ray Bulger for Slime Balls wheels from Santa Cruz

ATTITUDE

By now, you know skating is *intense*. That's why safety is an important part of a skater's mind-set. As with most other demanding sports, skateboarding isn't just a matter of using your body—the mind comes first. Think of it this way:

Skateboarding is body logic applied by the brain to air and terrain.

Rippin' is a great way for people to come to terms with themselves. When there's nothing out there but the street and the zzzzz of your wheels, you can think.

You can feel free. Grab on to what's bothering you.

Skateboarding often comes along at a time in your life when you're developing a new sense of self. Maybe you're relying less on parents, teachers, and counselors. You feel a sense of freedom, and a little bit of fear about what's next. Skating helps you deal with the present—and with the future. You'll find time to think about where you're going, and what you're doing.

Skating takes commitment and work. Even when horsing around on your board, you're usually working on things. Maybe perfecting a trick. Or mastering a hill. Whatever the task, you're adding your own intensity.

That's what makes superior skating impossible for druggies and hardcore punks. For them, a board is at best an accessory. So if you've never had a brain

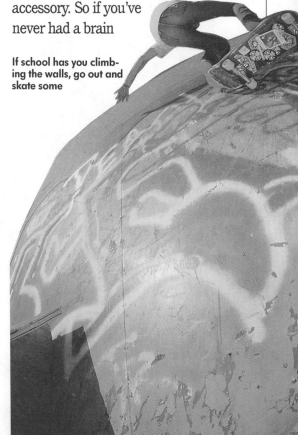

If school has you climbing the walls, go out and skate some

to begin with—or worse, damaged it with chemicals—stay off a board. It's too dangerous for people out of control.

Even skateboarding has its problem personalities—skaters with an attitude. "Attitude" in skating usually means some dude thinks he's so flamin' rad that nobody's good enough to skate with him. Or talk to him.

Bad attitude has been around since long before the urethane wheel. Since before the wheel itself, in fact. So just roll around it.

Attitude may be one factor that keeps more women from skating. Some guys make it tough for women to get rolling, calling them Sheilas, Board Bettys, or wenches. Sound derisive? They mean it that way.

Maybe that's why girls generally aren't into skating. Many like to hang with skaters, but few embrace the sport. Even in places where skating is big, there's just a handful of women on boards.

Let's hope this changes. Women add another dimension to any human activity. Not to mention that spark of sexuality. So if you're female and reading this, here's an invitation: Join the sport. Make it better.

The best skatewear is whatever works for you—sometimes flashy, always functional

STYLE

Like boards, trucks, and wheels, skatewear is made for the skater in motion. It's anti-establishment, but with style. It can be a reflection of your own taste, or a playback of someone else's esthetic vision.

Most skaters are into an action look because it works. And the graphics match their feelings. Open shirts, or no shirt. T-shirts with skate logos. Bright prints. Baggies or jams. Two or three-toned hi-tops.

Some skaters exhibit the death-warmed-over look—skulls, blood, bones, and gore. That's fine, 'cause nobody seems intimidated. Remember that skating is liberation; that's the way it's supposed to be.

Grab fast—and watch the sky fly by

Skateboarding is relatively safe. You can keep it that way by using common sense and taking care of your equipment. Sure, you can wipe out on a skateboard. But you can do the same walking across the street. Just work on getting the right attitude. Once you've got it, there ain't any more rules.

TRANSPORTATION

Skateboarding is a superior means of transportation. Why take your Chevy to the levee when you can make the trek with your deck? Getting there is more than half the fun, and never in the history of skateboarding have so many people agreed. That's because skateboarding is more than a way to get from Point A to Point B—it's an expressionistic form of tranportation that reflects what's going on inside of you.

Let's say you're on your way to school. With books in a book bag and board in hand, you walk out the door, hit the pavement, and roll. Your "run" to school might include 180s up curbs and ollies over something as small as a sidewalk crack, or as big as a trash can.

Many skaters steer clear of sidewalks when using their boards for transportation. Why? Well, the street is hard to beat. Streets are smoother and offer more room as long as you have a healthy respect for traffic hazards. A devoted skateboarder who's just heading out to a friend's house might do dozens of maneuvers along the way, turning the trip into a mini-jam session.

True, if you're doing distance on a straightaway route, the trip might be taken at top speed, sans diversions. But if it's a short jaunt, survey the area and skate what's around, such as driveways, ledges, embankments, and steps. *Anything* can happen along the way: power slides, coper grinds on curbs (especially metal-edged curbs, *the smoothest*), ollies over curbs and obstacles,

inverts, or even jumping over the neighbor's dog.

Challenge yourself. Ollie down three or four steps, or rail slide a handrail. If you're good, try wall rides at the parking lots and buildings you pass. Stucco's better than bricks, because of the smoothness. Ever skate with a bag of groceries (including three dozen eggs) and test how high you can ollie? Life gets interesting. The harder the ride, the more fun for the rider.

Give yourself a treat. Skating a new neighborhood can get you stoked. Do some ripping while you wait at the bus stop. And don't forget the shredder's transit advantage: a skateboard is always an available seat while waiting for the bus.

Walls, curbs, park benches—anything's fair game en route for Jeff Hartsel

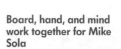

Board, hand, and mind work together for Mike Sola

Don't overlook another practical, if unglamorous, use: your board can help you take out the garbage. Roll the cans along on top of your board. Do your trashin' while thrashin'.

HILLS 'N SPILLS

Skating uphill isn't a problem—it's just tiring. You have to really push hard, but it's good conditioning, and getting your legs in shape will pay off when you turn to ramp or other forms of skating.

Skating downhill can be fast—too fast. From a safety standpoint, "too fast" is any time you're moving faster than you can bail. Yeah, some skaters ignore their personal speed limit. But most would rather live to read their next copy of *Thrasher.* How do you slow down on a steep incline? By sliding (skidding sideways) or by dragging your back foot. People also slow down on hills and at corners by slapping the ground with their Vans, Visions, Airwalks, or plain old sneaks. Better have a shoe replacement fund, though.

Jason Urbisci catches some air

DOING DISTANCE

Some skaters attempt long distances when they're not in a hurry to get where they're going. Like going uphill, it's a great way to condition your legs. If the weather's good, skating 30 to 50 blocks can be a breeze. Even without a board, the confirmed thrasher unconsciously skates the territory—then returns to execute his mental rips.

Once in awhile there's a mass skate trek of 20 miles or so as skaters session everything along the way. And some better neighborhoods may be the target of "pool searches" as skaters comb the terrain for waterless pools to ride.

Doing distance is mainly a leg event. It's better with other skaters around for company and inspiration, and more fun in good weather, when the road's an invitation to rip.

Doing distance sometimes means finding the best obstacles for intense sessions

Great terrain brings out the best in every skater

Skateboarding has arrived as a creative way of going places. And this generation is the first to see it. Maybe when today's 15-year-olds become tomorrow's commuters, we'll have skateboarding lanes on highways and skateboard lockers at the office.

WORKING STIFFS

In lots of places around the country, newspapers are delivered by skateboarders. Bag over shoulder, they cruise and toss until the route is done, then skate on to the local jammin' scene. It sure beats the bike-lying-in-the-dirt routine.

Young people skate to all kinds of jobs on boards. Even the not-so-young cling to their boards—and youth—when commuting. At least one Philadelphia stockbroker skates to work, tucking his tie into his shirt so it doesn't flop up in his face. Think it affects his performance? Do a Benihana, invest in Nissan; a few airwalks, and drop a hundred grand on Boeing.

Smith grind by Jeff Hartsel

TRICKS

CHAPTER 5

ricks are a natural part of skateboarding. They are the skater's self-expression—one individual, one board, flowing together in controlled motion. Perfecting your moves may be a solitary experience, but skateboarding isn't really a solo sport. It's meant to be shared. So show your stuff—it can be the spark that fires the imagination of another skater.

This chapter doesn't attempt to catalog every trick that's ever been skated. Since skateboarding reinvents itself daily, that would be impossible. There are hundreds, maybe thousands, of tricks done all over the world. Some stay local and never make it out of Boise, Idaho. Others travel the globe through contests, magazines, videos—even informal jams at international airports. And that's great, because passin' it on is what skateboarding is all about.

So here's my contribution—a basic guide to today's tricks. The list below isn't a lawbook; it's an idea book. Study it until you find yourself saying, "Yeah. I think I'll try that one now!"

These tricks are arranged in approximate order of difficulty, so you have the option of mastering them one by one as they become progressively harder. They are organized somewhat arbitrarily into three categories: street, freestyle, and vertical. Sometimes, you'll see overlap because many tricks are built on basic moves. So if you find a trick that looks out of place, don't sweat it—just skate it!

Everybody bails when learning new tricks. It's part of the process. But what shouldn't be part of the game is unnecessary injury. *Don't attempt these tricks without protective gear appropriate to the trick.* Get a helmet, gloves, pads for your knees, elbows, and wrists, hi-top shoes—

and don't leave 'em in the back of your closet; they can't help you there.

So that's safety first—terminology second. Let's talk basics. Even if you've had some experience, take time to review these terms because they're crucial to understanding the descriptions, especially of advanced tricks. Of course, body position—where you put your hands, your feet, your twirling torso—are key in doing most tricks. But you'll also see frequent reference to *transition* and *rails* in the following instructions.

A transition is a change in elevation—either up or down. It's the terrain in front of you. For example, the rising part of a launch or street ramp is a transition. Rails, as you learned in the equipment chapter, are an important accessory for the underside of your deck. But the term rail also means the side of your board. When you're told to grab the "frontside rail" you'll be grabbing the side of the board, and possibly the rails underneath, if that's comfortable for you.

Now we'll put you on the board. Climb on and get ready to rip.

Everybody bails when trying new tricks, so wear protective gear

Regular stance

Choose the stance that's comfortable for you— either regular or goofy foot

Goofy foot stance

STANCE

When it comes to basic riding stance, nothing is etched in stone. Do what you like. Skateboarding is freedom on wheels. But if you're just starting out, it helps to know what most people do. For example, a skater taking his basic ride often goes *goofy-foot*, which means riding or doing a trick with your right foot forward toward the nose of the board. *Regular stance* is the mirror opposite of this—left foot on the nose, right foot on the tail.

Hands

You have to understand which hand is being referred to in order to follow trick instructions. This is especially true of grabs, which are all-important in this sport.

Backside Hand. Your backside hand is your lead or forward hand, closest to the nose.

Frontside Hand. This is your trailing hand, closest to the tail.

Backside hand

Frontside hand

Frontside ollie by Rick 'Spidy' DeMontrond

Turns

Backside. In regular stance—with your left foot on the nose—this is a right, or clockwise, turn. When you're turning and going up a transition, your "backside" faces the transition.

Frontside. In regular stance, this is a left, or counterclockwise, turn.

Grabs

Crail. A grab with your frontside hand on the nose.

Nose. A grab with your backside hand on the nose.

Indy. A frontside grab on the frontside rail when you're turning backside.

Lien. A backside grab on the backside rail when you're turning frontside. This was developed and named for skater Neil Blender; it's "Neil" spelled backside.

Mute. A grab across your body with your backside hand on the frontside rail.

Stale. A grab across your body with your frontside hand on the backside rail.

Practice basic maneuvers before tackling tougher tricks

STREETSTYLE

Streetstyle, or street skating, means skating literally anywhere–wherever you want to go, put your board to it! The best board for streetstyle is a mini-board, which is slightly smaller than the deck you'd choose for vertical tricks. It measures about $9\frac{3}{4}'' \times 29\frac{1}{2}''$, although many skaters use vert and street boards interchangeably. Here are the basic fundamentals of street tricks:

Compressing. Learn to compress–bend at the knees–to maintain balance. Pumping–rhythmic compressing and rising–is a good way to pick up speed. This crouch also helps in some tricks and varies from slight to deep depending on the maneuver.

Kick-turn. An abrupt turn made by kicking down on your kicktail with your back foot, which lifts up the nose. Turn your body in the new direction you want to head while the nose is still in the air.

Tic-Tac. Turning left and right in rapid succession with a series of kick-turns. Tic-tacs can get you going without putting a foot on the ground.

Bert. Named after '70s skate pioneer Larry Bertleman. Turn 180 degrees by planting your backside hand on the ground behind you, sliding the tail out, and returning the way you came. Don't forget your gloves.

Basic Bert by Mike Garcia

Grind or *Slappy Grind.* Grinds require intense control of your body and the board. Learning them now will make it easier for you to pick up ollie/grind combinations and other tricks.

A grind is any trick where you ride up to a curb, lip, or coping (rounded edge) and grind your axles on that surface. It makes a kind of a "slap" as you hit the curb—hence, slappy grind. A curb is a decent place to start:

1. Approach the curb at about a 45-degree angle.
2. Keep both feet on the side of the board that's farthest from the grinding surface and raise your wheels on the curb side.
3. Shift your weight so you arrive on top of the curb.
4. Grind both axles and you're doing a 50/50 grind. This can be done frontside or backside. If you grind just the nose, it's a new deal; just the rear truck, it's a back axle grind; if you grind the rail and back truck, it's a Smith grind.
5. Go back down nose first.

Mike Smith blazes through a pool grind

Frontside curb grind by Bill Danforth

Ollies

An *ollie* is an important, basic way of getting airborne by hitting the kicktail with your back foot. Your hands never touch the deck. Here are the basics, and variations on the theme.

Basic Ollie. Cruise, compress, jump with your board, and land. Invented by Alan Gelfand back in the late '70s. Here's how:

1. Cruise on any surface, usually going straight. Keep your front foot perpendicular to the board (toes toward frontside rail, if you're riding goofy-foot), behind the front truck. The back foot can be angled.
2. Compress your body into a slight crouch.
3. Jump up while snapping the tail off the ground by kicking down. The board comes up with you, nose first.
4. Level the board out by sliding your front foot up over the front truck and pushing down gently. The higher you jump, the higher you ollie!
5. Usually the board lands on both trucks at once.

Jason Urbisci ollies whenever and wherever he can

Christian Hosoi ollies higher than the average skater

Ollie from street ramp to street ramp by Colby Carter

Stairs are no obstacle when Jason Urbisci ollies

Ollie to 50/50. An ollie where you land with both trucks on the lip of a curb or other obstacle.

1. Skate and ollie, approaching the obstacle from an angle or at 90 degrees.
2. Land with your trucks on the lip. Maintain balance.
3. Press down on the kicktail and rotate off, keeping your board flat. Turning frontside, as with all ollies, usually is easier than turning backside.

Ollie to grind by Tony Magnusson

Ollie to Boardslide or ***Ollie to Railslide.*** Ollie up to a curb or other obstacle, land on your rails, and slide. Come down backward at 90 degrees.

Ollie to Back Axle. Same as ollie to 50/50, but all weight pivots on the back axle.

Half-Cab or ***180 Ollie.*** Same as regular ollie, only turn 180 degrees frontside or backside. As you twist, the board should stay with you. Land facing backward and continue in the same direction.

Ollie to Tail. Can be done on any obstacle with a lip, such as a bench or curb. Like a 180 ollie, only as you're positioned over the lip of your obstacle, direct the tail downward and land on it. Drop with the board flat and skate away! Can be done frontside or backside. A good street trick.

Ollie to 50/50 Grind. Same as ollie to 50/50, only keep the momentum going while landing on both axles. Approach the obstacle at an angle.

Ollie Nosepick. Approach obstacle at 90 degrees. Ollie up over the obstacle, landing on the front axle. Put all your weight on the front axle and rotate off fakie (the same way you came).

Homemade rails are what Mark Mannheimer slides

Shiftie. Like a regular ollie, only you shift the board's direction in mid-air. Land on back wheels and continue—tail forward—in same direction you originally were going. Can be done backside or frontside.

Ollie to Grab. An ollie to a grab in any desired way—let your imagination roam on this one.

Ollie Wallride. From vertical, to horizontal, to vertical—with a little ollie magic.
1. Approach the wall at a slight angle, either frontside or backside.
2. Ollie up onto the wall, landing on both sets of wheels and skating the wall.
3. Shift your weight. Push down with your front foot and slide the front wheels off the wall first, then the back wheels. You're pushing the board down and away.
4. Land on all wheels and skate away.

Ollie Kick-flip. An ollie where you kick-flip (see Freestyle) a whole rotation and land normally, going the same direction.
1. Skate and ollie.
2. Slide your front foot off the board, while kicking downward on the

Ollie to grab by Jeff Phillips

backside edge. This makes the board flip side-over-side.
3. As the board flips, bring your knees up above the board. Put both feet back on the board after the rotation.
4. Land going in the same direction.

Ollie Flip to Axle. This is a very hard street trick. Same as ollie to back axle, except with a kick-flip. Land on one or both axles.

Caballerial or **360 Ollie.** A complete spin in the air, frontside or backside. Like a gay twist (see Advanced Tricks) with no grab. Invented by pro Steve Caballero. *Warning: Consult your local ollie guru before attempting this difficult trick.*

A launch ramp or quarter pipe puts you on the wall

John Thomas launches into a boneless and catches some air

Boneless

A *boneless* trick is done with one foot on the ground. You grab with your frontside hand on the frontside rail and kick off the ground with your front foot. Named by skater G.S.D. (Gary Scott Davis) after his toy doll, "the boneless one."

Backside Boneless. Place your backside hand on the back rail and push off the ground with your front foot. Get in the air, then put your front foot back on the board and land.

Boneless 180. Grab with your frontside hand on the frontside rail, thrust your front foot down onto the ground. Spin 180 degrees, land, and roll backward—in the same direction that you originally were going.

Boneless 360. Same as above, but spin 360 degrees.

Backside boneless by Keith Hershman

360 Slide. A frontside or backside slide 360 done without grabbing the board. This also can be done layback style (with a hand on the ground—don't forget those gloves).

Tail Slide. Ollie or air (see Airs, page 66) to an obstacle. Land on the tail, maintain momentum, and slide on it.

A slice of action in a 360 judo air

Randy Colvin rail slides a ramp coping

Slides

A *slide* is any maneuver where you slide out your tail, with the back wheels skidding as you change direction 90 degrees or more.

Street Airs

There are many, many street airs. Most of these are also done in vertical skating and are detailed later in this chapter. Here's a handful of airs often seen in the street:

360 Air. Usually done off a launch ramp. Do an airborne 360-degree spin by twisting your arms and torso. While flying, hold the board frontside, backside, or mute.

360 Judo Air. Also done off a launch ramp, this is simply a 360 air done while kicking your front foot out judo style.

Rocket Air. Can be done off a street ramp or on vert.

1. Ride up the transition and launch, grabbing backside on the back rail toward the nose.
2. Put your front foot on the tail while you're in the air. Grab the front rail close to the nose with your frontside hand.
3. Arch your back, so you and the board together make a triangle.
4. To land, just slide your foot back and come down as in a regular air.

Christ Air or **Christ Noldair.** Fly through the air looking like a crucifix launched by NASA. Named after creators and perfectors Christian Hosoi and Monty Nolder. Here's how:

1. Ride up the transition and launch.
2. Grab the nose backside, then throw out your arms (with one hand still holding the board) to form a T-shape with your body. Your legs point down.
3. Reposition the board under you and land.

Christ air by Christian Hosoi

NASA can't match this rocket air by Christian Hosoi

Other Street Moves

Bomb Drop. An old trick where you pick up your board, hold it in your hand, drop off something (like a car), land on your board, and skate away!

Shove-It. Ride and snap the board upward a bit, as in an ollie. Use your back foot to sweep the board clockwise, pushing it along the back edge and spinning 180 or 360 degrees. Land and continue skating.

Tailspin. A complete 360-degree spin on the tail. Ride along, take your front foot off the deck, and pivot back on your tail while pushing around with your front foot so you spin 360 degrees.

Street Sadplant. Invert (see Handplants or Inverts below) with front leg extended on board.

1. Place your backside hand on the frontside of the board.
2. Plant your other hand behind yourself on the ground while taking your feet off the board.
3. Put the board over your head while pushing your feet up into the air, also over your head.
4. While inverted, put your feet back on the board. Extend your front leg on the nose and briefly lock your knee.
5. Pull the board back under your body, put both feet on, and roll back in.

See Vertical Skating later in this chapter for more ideas about inverts and street skating.

Christian Hosoi
handplants streetstyle

Freestyle tricks are done with a shorter, narrower board—usually 7″ × 27″, the kicktail is flatter than on a street or ramp board. You'll want a smaller truck so the wheels are flush with the side of the board for balancing tricks. The front truck is farther back from the end of the nose, giving you more room up front. There are no side cuts.

In freestyle competitions, you usually have one to two minutes to do your run. Your challenge is to flow—to stay on the board, not fall, and do difficult, stylish tricks. You're evaluated on the basis of difficulty, balance (not falling), and style. Variation counts, too. In other words, ten different kinds of handstands aren't as good as ten different tricks.

Competition Tips

1. Be dedicated. Skate often by yourself and polish your performance style.
2. Practice to the music you'll use in competition. Get into the music; make your runs seem like part of it.
3. Don't think about the crowd. After you've mastered your tricks, skate in front of people; you'll draw a crowd if you're any good. Get some attention now so you don't get stage fright come contest time.

Here are some tricks to get you on your way to freestyle fun. All you need is a board, a patch of land, and a can-do attitude. So just keep rolling.

Daffy. An ancient trick done on two boards. Your lead foot does a tail wheelie (see Wheelies, below), and your trailing foot does a nose wheelie. Adding a turn makes this more interesting.

V-Sit. Another old-fashioned trick that you just might want to try for people who haven't seen it. Here, you end up holding the sides of the board, with your legs together and pointing up at an angle. Your bottom is off the deck. To V-sit, simply sit on your board and pop into the V! Easiest done rolling.

Kick-Flip. Skate, move both feet to the board's center, then edge the toes of your front foot under the backside rail. Pull up with your toes, jump as the board flips side-over-side beneath you, and then land back on it!

Spacewalk. Like a tic-tac, but your front wheels don't touch the ground. Use your arms and legs to achieve a back-and-forth motion of the board's nose.

Yo-yo. A very hard trick also done on the street. This is an invert without touching your foot to the ground. Ride backward, plant your frontside hand, and grab like a regular invert. Use your momentum to thrust your body up into the inverted position.

G-turn

Wheelies

A *wheelie* is any trick where you balance on one set of wheels. The key is in balancing your entire body at once—head, arms, torso, and legs.

Nose Wheelie. Get your front foot at an angle across the deck, over the front wheels. Your back foot is on the tail or over the back truck. Arch your body forward, bend your back knee, and balance your arms. You're doing it!

Nose Wheelie Spacewalk. Do a nose wheelie and roll back and forth in S-shaped turns without letting your back wheels touch the ground.

G-Turn. Do a nose wheelie and turn off to the left or right more than 180 degrees. This can be a tighter and tighter spiral, or looser and looser. G-turns often lead into 360s and other tricks.

Nose Wheelie 360. This means, as it says, doing a 360 off the nose. Foot positioning can vary, but the easiest is regular riding position, with one foot on the nose and one on the tail.

One-wheeled Wheelie. You'll need medium to tight trucks—this trick is impossible to do with loose trucks. Do a nose or tail wheelie and lean forward or backward onto one wheel. This trick usually is done in a straight line. For a difficult variation, try a one-wheeled G-turn.

Tail Wheelie. Put your back foot across the tail and your front foot at an angle just behind the front truck. Extend your arms, bend your knees, and you're into it.

Two-footed Wheelie. Can be done with two feet on nose or tail. Balance your feet across the trucks, facing in the direction of the board. Bend your knees, extend your arms, and wheelie. This is harder to do when stationary.

Tail wheelie by Mike Sola

One-wheeled wheelie by Mike Sola

Two-footed wheelie

50/50

Doing a *50/50* is like half of a kick-flip, where the board ends up upside down, with your front foot under the board and your back foot on top of the underside of the tail. A kick-flip is not absolutely necessary to get into the final 50/50 position —some skaters get there from pogos and other tricks.

50/50–Freestyle
1. Put your back foot under the frontside edge of the tail.
2. Put your front foot in the direction of the board, behind the front truck and on the backside rail.
3. Simultaneously push down on your front foot and scoop up the underside of the board with your back foot.
4. Flip the board toward yourself–side over side–as you jump.
5. The nose covers your front foot, and your back foot rests on the underside of the tail.

Caspers

A *casper* is done standing on your rail as the board balances on its side and the side of the wheels. Use your front foot to kick the deck in the direction you want to spin–either 180 or 360 degrees.

Casper 50/50. Essentially a stationary balancing trick. Start with a basic casper and slip your foot down to the back wheels. Lift up the nose and balance on the edge of the tail. You usually don't spin in a 50/50 casper, unless you're super-talented.

Casper Spacewalk. Get into your basic casper 50/50 and spacewalk.

Basic handstand

Handstands

Handstands can be done standing on your board or on the ground; starting on the ground is easier. Do this slowly at first until you gain confidence. For variation, try a one-armed handstand.

Handstand
1. Grab the nose with your backside hand, and the tail with your frontside hand.
2. Run alongside your board.
3. Kick your legs up into a handstand.
4. Come back down with your legs between your hands and land on the board.

Handstand Kick-flip. This is a kick-flip only in the sense that your hands are doing what your feet usually do in a kick-flip–turning the board over. This is often done while rolling; stationary is harder.
1. Get into a handstand position on the board.
2. Curl your fingers around the sides (rails) of the board.
3. Flip the board beneath yourself (360 degrees side-over-side) while thrusting your body up with your arms.

4. Grab the rails as soon as the board flips and maintain your handstand.
5. Land with both feet on the deck.

Press to Handstand. Do a handstand while rolling very low and close to the ground. Press upward (like an overhead press in weight lifting) to a full handstand. Land with both feet on the deck as in a regular handstand.

Handstand Pogo. Get into a one-footed pogo. Bend over and put your frontside hand where your foot was. Put your backside hand on the nose. Thrust your legs up and hop. Even the pros manage only about two hops with this difficult trick.

Handstand Wheelie. This one's harder than it looks on paper.
1. Do a handstand.
2. Lift your front wheels off the ground.
3. Roll on your back wheels.
4. Put your front wheels back down to the ground, and return your feet to the deck.

Pogos

Pogos are balancing and hopping tricks done on the tail. They were inspired by the once-popular pogo stick.

Pogo
1. Do a tail stall by raring back on the tail and grabbing the nose.
2. Finger-flip the board 180 degrees. Land your back foot on your back truck.
3. Hug the top of the deck with your other leg in pogo stick fashion.
4. Hop and use your arms for balance.
5. Easiest way back down: finger-flip the board 180 and land.

One-footed Pogo. Get into standard pogo position. Grab the nose with one or two hands. Bend your front foot back for balance and hop.

![VERTICAL TRICKS]

Vertical skating tricks have been the cutting edge of skateboarding as the sport pushes on toward middle age. Vert is where skaters get the most air—and the most freedom. Be sure to wear proper protective gear, 'cause you can skate with a cracked board, but not a cracked brain.

Many vertical tricks can be done on a quarter-pipe or a half-pipe. In fact, there's a great deal of overlap with street skating—a lot of tricks can be practiced on launch or quarter-pipes if a big ramp just ain't around.

Let's begin with a couple of basic tricks that are a part of skating on transitional surfaces:

Ramps, walls, pipes, pools—skate whatever's available

Carving a popular pool

Carves

Carving goes back to one of the original great transitional surfaces: a pool. Many of the ingredients in today's tricks were first developed in these aquamarine wonderlands.

Carve. Riding up a transition and turning 180 without taking your wheels off the ground. Essentially, you're carving a "C" shaped path. Carving sometimes means drifting in the air across the top of the ramp.

Carve Grinding. Carving up to a lip and coming back down at 90 degrees. This is mainly done in pools.

Backside carve grind by Tony Alva

One-footed Carve. An old school trick that can be done in a pool. Do a frontside or backside carve while lifting your back foot off the board—usually raising it behind you.

Airs

Air is critical to life—and to skateboarding. We move through it, above it, around it—gaining and losing contact with the ground at our own willful discretion.

So what is an "air"? You can tell your chemistry teacher that it's not just a beaker filled with common nitrogen, oxygen, and rarer gases. An *air* is any trick that gets you airborne while grabbing the deck. Award your favorite skating sticker to any teach who accepts this definition of "air."

Airs of all kinds are a big dimension in modern skating. Airs deliver freedom from gravity and liberation from the bounds of terrain. So take your air often. It's a skater's vitamins.

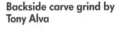

Frontside air by John Lucero

Beginner Airs

Master the following six airs before attempting more ambitious moves. You'll be able to use them in combinations, possibly creating your own unique contribution to the art of airs.

Frontside Air. Any air done with your chest facing the upgrade of the transition. One hand grabs the deck at least briefly.

1. Hand: Frontside.
2. Grab: Frontside rail between legs.
3. Direction of turn: Frontside.

A thrilling backside air by Joe Johnson

Backside Air. Any air with your back facing the upgrade of the transition. (Remember that you're positioned sideways on the board; you're not literally riding backward when turning backside.)

1. Hand: Backside.
2. Grab: Back rail close to your lead foot.
3. Direction of turn: Backside.

Slob Air. Nothing sloppy about this maneuver. Before catching air, grab the frontside rail with your backside hand. Turn frontside, land, and release.

1. Hand: Backside.
2. Grab: Between legs on frontside rail.
3. Direction: Frontside.

Justin Girard does a neat slob air

Indy air by Eric Nash

Eric Nash rips into a
mute air

Indy Air. A backside air with a frontside grab on the frontside rail.
1. Hand: Frontside.
2. Grab: Between legs on frontside rail.
3. Direction: Backside.

Mute Air. A backside air done with a backside grab on the frontside rail.
1. Hand: Backside.
2. Grab: Frontside rail across your body and around your front knee.
3. Direction: Backside.

Lien Air. A frontside air grabbing backside on the backside rail.
1. Hand: Backside.
2. Grab: Backside rail close to the heel of your lead foot.
3. Direction: Frontside.

Lien air by Robert Torres

Frontside Air Variations

Tailbone Air, Boned Frontside Air, or *Nosebone Frontside Air.* A cool-looking air, no matter what you call it. This is the same as a regular frontside air, but with your front leg boned (extended):

1. Grab the frontside rail with your frontside hand.
2. Spin the tail out in front of you. Bone your back leg out in front of your body and keep it straight.
3. Return to normal position and land as your board does a 180. Re-enter like a normal frontside air.

Back Leg Straight Frontside Air. Same as a regular frontside air, but as the name says—with your back leg pointed straight back. Grab closer to the nose.

Frigid Frontside Air. Do a frontside air, but pull your front foot off the board and put it down in the air. Put your foot back on the board and drop in.

Frontside Tuck-knee Air. Grab frontside snugly around your tucked back leg. Tweak (arch your body) and land.

Boned frontside air by
Chris Miller

Backside Air Variations

Judo Air. In this air, you kick your front leg out—almost as if attacking some mysterious gremlin beside you! Here's how:

1. Ride into your transition and launch.
2. Grab the back rail with your backside hand.
3. Kick out your front foot.
4. Return your foot to the board, release grip, and land.

Jason Urbisci puts the shoe on you with a judo air

Frigid to Judo Air or ***Pendulum Air.*** In one motion, do a judo, a frigid, and get back on the board.

Japan Air. A mute air where you tuck both knees downward. Grab frontside of the board around and under your knee.

Neon (Knee On). In this air, you pick up your front foot and plant your front knee on the deck while turning backside.

Alley Oop Backside Air. Carve up the transition frontside, then grab and do a backside air grabbing backside on the back rail. Spin in the opposite direction of your turn.

Alley Oop Mute. Carve up the wall for a frontside air and grab mute. While you're in the air, turn backside 180 and drop in.

Backside Air to Axle. Alley oop a backside air and land with both axles on the coping.

Varial. Grab the board with your lead hand on the back rail while going up backside. As you're into the turn, spin 180 degrees and land with board facing backward (tail first). Roll on down.

This UFO is Kevin Staab, lighting the sky with a neon air

Japan air by Sergie Ventura

Frigid air by Mike Sola

Frigid Air. An air in which you kick your front leg off the board out at an angle behind your body. This is similar to a judo air, except that your leg is thrust out in the opposite direction.

Soaring into a 747 is Mike Sola

Other Air Variations

Tucked Slob Air. Turn frontside and grab mute around your tucked knee.

Back Leg Straight Slob Air. Regular slob air, with back leg extended.

Tucked Indy Air. Tucked knee with a grab around the knee.

Boned Indy Air. Done with your front leg straight.

747. A tucked Indy air–but tweak your body!

Klingon. A one-footed mute air. Start with a mute air–take your back foot off and straighten it down. Return your foot to the board and drop back in.

Airwalk. An air where you grab the nose with your backside hand and kick out in different directions with both legs. Your front foot kicks judo, and your back foot kicks frigid.

Lien Airwalk. Use a backside grab on the backside rail while turning frontside and doing an airwalk.

Method air by Eddie
Elguera

Method Air. An air in which you grab your back rail with your backside hand while turning backside. Keep your legs parallel with the ground.

Crossbone. A lien air where you take your board and use it like a windshield wiper! Swing the tail out in front while keeping your feet on the board, then bring it back and proceed down the transition.

Finger-flip Air. Nose grab with a finger-flip in the air.

1. Ride up the transition and launch into a backside turn.
2. Grab the nose with your backside hand.
3. Pull your feet up while keeping the board underneath your body.
4. Flip the board one complete rotation.
5. Land and roll away!

Crossbone by Chris
Miller

Finger-flip
lien to tail by
Jason Jessee

Lip Tricks

These tricks usually are done on the lip or coping of a half-pipe, quarter-pipe, or pool. But many also are done on street, using a curb or another handy transition.

Dropping In. Put your tail on the coping and lean in gently while compressing.

Axle Stall. Kick-turn up, land both axles on the lip, and stall (stop). Drop back in at 90 degrees.

Rock-n-Roll. Roll up to a lip. Land with your front truck on the deck or other side of the lip, and your back truck up against the coping but still inside the transition. Kick-turn by putting pressure on the tail —usually turning backside—and come back down the transition.

Frontside Rock-n-Roll. This one's tough. Go up frontside, do a rock-n-roll, and come back in. Keeping your balance is difficult for most beginners.

Nosepick. A trick where you turn and your front truck lands on the coping, curb, or lip. Pivot 90 degrees and roll in nose first. Variations include the ollie nosepick and frontside nosepick.

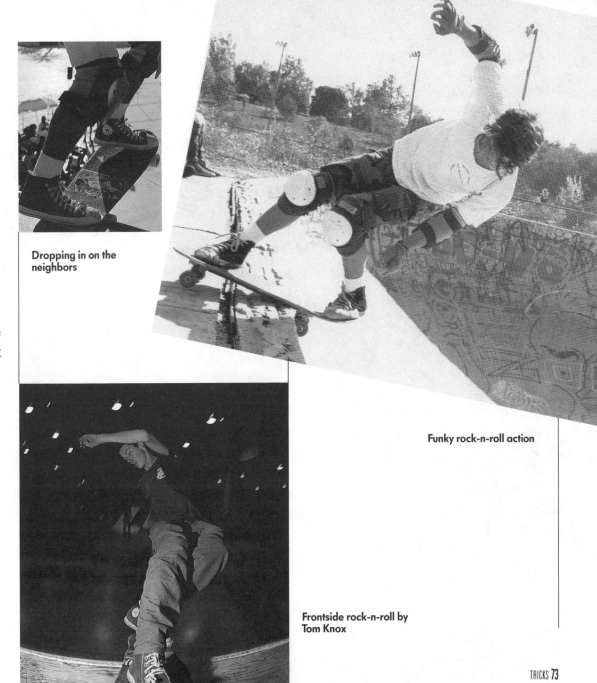

Dropping in on the neighbors

Funky rock-n-roll action

Frontside rock-n-roll by Tom Knox

Indy Nosepick. Do an Indy air–grab frontside, turn backside. Land on your front axle, pivot, and pull back into the transition at 90 degrees.

Rail Slide. Carve up the transition and lift your front wheels over the coping. Distribute your weight evenly and slide on your rails. Finish like a rock-n-roll, nose first.

Tail Slide. Do a lien air, getting very little air. Put the tail on the coping and use the momentum to slide yourself along as far as you can before dropping back in.

Crail Slide. Like a tail slide, but with a crail grab–frontside hand on the nose.

Revert. After performing an air or lip trick, add some style with a revert. Right after landing, do a quick 180 slide so you're heading backward (fakie). Also called a reverse re-entry.

Sundown doesn't slow down a dedicated rail slider

Frontside tail sliding for the crowd

Indy nosepick by Monty Nolder

Crail slide by Greg Aguilar

74

There's nothing laid-back about Bill Danforth's layback rollout

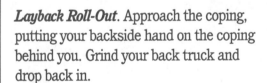

Frontside 50/50 grind by Richard Zuccarello

Thrashers like Bill Tocco don't avoid disaster—they skate it

Layback Roll-Out. Approach the coping, putting your backside hand on the coping behind you. Grind your back truck and drop back in.

50/50 Grind. Carve up the transition, putting both axles on the coping, like an axle stall. Grind across the coping on both axles and drop in nose first.

Disaster. A vert or street ramp trick where you do an ollie air 180, land lapped over the coping, push your nose down and come back down.

Backside 50/50 grind by Erik Castro

Invert by Steve Schneer

Layback air by Chris Livingston

Handplants or Inverts

In vertical skating, *inverts* or *handplants* are a big part of the game. Handplants seem to come in the most varieties—maybe this means the future is upside-down!

Invert. Turn backside, grabbing with your backside hand between your legs. Plant your frontside hand on the coping and thrust up your body. Once up, stall on your arm. Fall back in nose first, pushing off with your hand as you pass the coping.

Lay Air or *Layback Air.* An invert done as follows:

1. Approach coping, turning slightly frontside.
2. Grab mute (backside hand on the front rail).
3. Plant your frontside hand on the lip.
4. Do a simultaneous handplant and a frontside 180. (Many skaters don't get completely inverted.)
5. Keep your weight on your arm as you twist around in a frontside direction.
6. Land and proceed back down the transition.

Varial invert by Joe Johnson

Smith Vert. This is an invert with your legs twisted. Grab mute, invert and briefly twist your board and feet one-quarter turn backside while upside down. Bring the board back under you and drop down.

Tuck-knee Invert. This differs from other inverts because of your knee position. Your backside hand grabs mute around your front leg. Go inverted and arch your back. This is a basic kind of invert, but it can be extreme depending on how much you arch your back or tuck your knee.

Andrecht. An invert where you grab the back rail with your backside hand. Named after '70s skater Dave Andrecht.

Stale Vert or **Stalemasky.** An Andrecht where you grab the back rail by reaching through your legs.

Bonedrecht or **Sad Andrecht.** An Andrecht while boning out your front leg.

Sad Andrecht by Jeff Hedges

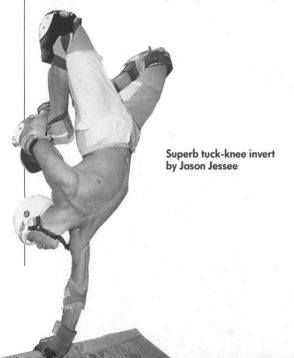

Superb tuck-knee invert by Jason Jessee

Andrecht handplant by Christian Hosoi

Sadplant *(vertical version).* This is an invert done with the front leg extended on the board.

1. Go up the transition.
2. Grab with your backside hand on frontside of the board. Place your back hand on the coping. You'll almost automatically be inverted if you keep your momentum going.
3. Once inverted, extend your front leg on the nose. The back leg remains bent and on board.
4. To go back down, pull board underneath your body and descend.

One Footer. A simple variation on a basic. Do an invert and take your back foot off the deck.

Gymnast. Do an invert and take both feet off the deck.

Switcharoo. An invert in which you switch your grab position from the back rail to the front rail. Do a stale invert, grabbing through your legs on the backside rail, then switch your grab to the frontside rail.

Channel Plant or **Channel Invert.** An air over the channel followed by an invert after the cross-over. A channel is a curved trough cut vertically into the top of some ramps to let you roll in.

One-footed invert by Bill Tocco

Eddie Elguera casts sadplant magic in a bowl

Frontside invert over the channel by Steve Schneer

Gymnast plant by
Jeff Ferris

Ho-ho draws smiles—
this street trick can be
done at the lip

Frontside invert by Claus
Grabke

Hip Hop. An invert where you plant your hand on one side of the channel and then on the other. You'll be hoppin' on your hand.

Ho-Ho. Invert, followed by handstand (balance the board on your feet), followed by an eggplant. Begin with your backside hand on the board, end with your frontside hand on the board. You'll find endless variations: Bone your front leg out; hang the board off your front foot; do what feels good.

Frontside Invert. Turn frontside, plant your backside (lead) hand on the coping, and grab straight down on the front rail with your frontside hand. For variety, try a tuck-knee invert or a sad frontside invert.

Clothespin Invert or *Pervert.* An invert where you place the board between your knees or thighs. Squeeze and hold it. Grab the board and re-enter, feeling stupid.

Eggplants

Eggplant. Same as an invert or hand-plant, but with an opposite grab. In other words, grab with your frontside hand on the front rail as you plant your backside hand on the coping and invert.

Tuck-knee Eggplant. An eggplant where you grab regular frontside snugly around your back knee, forcing it down into a tuck.

Sad Eggplant. An eggplant where you straighten your front leg.

Eggdrecht. An eggplant where you grab the back rail.

Fakie

Whenever you're riding tail first, you're rippin' *fakie.* Some tricks lend themselves to a fakie return, such as airs, ollies, rock-n-rolls, or inverts. Just do the manuever and come down backward (tail first). Other tricks start with you traveling fakie up the transition. Here's a few (and all can be done nose forward, too):

Fakie Tail Stall. Ride up the transition fakie, and when your tail comes to the coping, lean upward and grab the nose of your board. Pivot upward on your tail and drop back in.

Fakie Smith Stop or *Fakie Smith Stall.* Ride up the transition fakie and put your back truck on the coping. Pivot so that your rail is also on the coping with your nose pointed down at an angle. Stall on your back truck and rail, then compress and drop in.

Thruster. A boneless done at the top of a ramp to give you some quick, clean air. Here's how:
1. Ride up fakie.
2. Grab the tail with your frontside hand.
3. Take your back foot off the board and plant it on the coping or lip.
4. Thrust up and come back down in normal riding position, facing forward.

Good Buddy. Ride up the transition fakie, do an eggplant, and then come back in nose first.

Fakie Ollie to Smith. This is a combination trick that's exactly what it says. Do an ollie from fakie. As you're coming down, place your back truck on the coping and your frontside rail on coping, in standard Smith position. Drop back in!

Fakie R-n-R Slider. Do a rock-n-roll rail slide and come back in fakie.

Eddie Reategui explores a full-pipe

Footplant by Jeff
Hartsel

Mute fastplant by 'Gator'

Footplants

Footplants are the vertical skater's way of gaining quick torque and momentum by thrusting off the lip or coping with his foot. It's like the streetstyle boneless, except done at the top of a ramp.

Sweeper

1. Do a lien air, but grabbing the nose with your backside hand while turning frontside.
2. Take your back foot off the deck as soon as you leave the coping.
3. Plant your back foot on the coping and pivot on your foot while sweeping your body around 180 degrees.
4. Land with the tail on the coping and nose in the air.
5. Put your back foot on the board and drop back in.

Paul Parry cleans up with
a sweeper

Texas Plant

1. Approach the lip grabbing mute, as if you're going to do a frontside air.
2. As soon as you're airborne, plant your back foot on the coping.
3. Grab the tail with your free hand—one hand mute and one on the tail.
4. Release your grip on the tail and re-plant your foot on board. Then re-enter.

Fast Plant. A footplant where you grab backside and place your back foot on the coping. Thrust up. Put your foot back on board.

Reverse bean plant by Jason Urbisci

Bean Plant. A kind of a boneless done in street or ramp skating, but in this one you grab backside in front of your front foot. Take your front foot off, plant it on the coping and thrust up, turning frontside. On a half-pipe or quarter-pipe, you turn 180 and end up riding nose forward. On the ground, you keep going straight.

Ice Plant. Go up the transition, do a bean plant, but turn backside.

Frontside Boneless. Ride up the transition and grab the front rail with your frontside hand between your legs. Take your front foot off, plant it on the coping, and turn 180 degrees frontside while pushing upward. Return your foot to the board and go back in.

Backside Boneless. Same as above, except grab with your backside hand on the back rail while turning 180 degrees backside.

Frontside boneless by Jeff Ferris

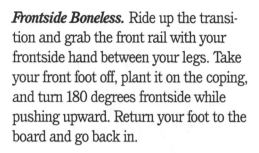

Indy Footplant. Grab indy and take your back foot off the deck. Plant it on the coping and jump back on and down.

Gatair or ***360 Fastplant.***
1. Ride up the ramp fakie.
2. Grab mute and spin like a gay twist (see Advanced Tricks, below).
3. As soon as you catch air, take your back foot off the board and thrust off the coping.
4. Complete the spin and re-enter.

Tricks to Tail

These tricks involve slapping the tail on the coping. Some common variations of tricks to tail include ollies (frontside and backside—backside being harder), fakie ollie, slob air, and frontside air.

Lien to Tail. Do a lien air, land with your tail on the coping, and drop-in.

Madonna. A lien frigid to tail. Go up the ramp like a frontside air, grab backside, kick your foot out frigid, and land your tail on the coping. Proceed down the transition. For variation, try the Sean Penn: backside frigid air to tail. (Film stars may quickly fade, but skaters usually stick with the names for their tricks.)

Madonna by Jon Steinberg

Backside boneless over the channel by C. Bewsey

Finger-Flip Lien to Tail. Another combination trick. Do a 360 finger-flip underneath your body during a lien air. Land on the tail and continue your skating extravaganza!

Switch-Hand Lien to Tail. A frontside air in which you switch from your frontside hand on the front rail to a backside hand nose-grab. Land on the tail, let go of the nose, and drop back in.

Body Jar. Do a backside air while grabbing the nose. Slap the tail down onto the coping and let go of the nose. Drop back in the transition.

Finger-flip lien to tail by
Chris Livingston

ADVANCED TRICKS

When you've graduated from the Academy of Advanced of Shredding, grab your diploma and try some of this post-doctoral work:

McTwist. A 540-degree spin in the air. On a ramp, you grab mute.
1. Ride up the transition, turning backside, and launch off the coping.
2. Grab mute (backside hand on frontside rail). Use your whole body to build momentum for the spin.
3. Spin backside.
4. Land proceeding forward down the transition.

McHawk. A 720 McTwist—two 360-degree spins back to back. Approach and launch as for a McTwist. Invented by Tony Hawk and done only by few others. Land and go down the transition fakie.

Gay Twist. Go up fakie, grab mute, spin 360 backside, and go back down as normal. In other words, this is a 360 air from fakie.

Phillips 66. A difficult vert trick popularized by Jeff Phillips. Sort of a 360 invert done at the lip.
1. Ride up fakie (tail first).
2. Grab the front rail with your backside hand, as in a regular invert.
3. Plant your frontside hand on the transition (the slanting part).
4. Thrust up, spin 360 degrees (rotating on your hand), and come down straight.

The Phillips 66 by its
creator—Jeff Phillips

It's a hurricane warning from 'Gator'

Benihana. A thruster in the air done on a half-pipe. Go up the transition fakie, grab the tail, kick your back foot out frigid. Put your foot back on the board and go back down the transition.

Hurricane. Go up to a rock-n-roll. Begin to turn frontside, so as to put your back axle and back rail on the coping. Stall there and rock back in backside, doing approximately a 270-degree spin. This can be done street as a hurricane grind on a curb.

Alley Oop 50/50 Grind. Come up toward the lip as if you're going to do a frontside air. Before the lip, turn backside to 50/50 grind, grind backward, turn backside, and roll down the transition.

Backside Smith Grind. Frontside Smith grinds are a lot more common than this trick. It's not spectacular, but it's not easy either. Just do a backside grind on your back axle. Getting your balance here is the hardest part—push your backside rail down against the lip. Then re-enter on the vertical surface.

Backside Smith grind by Monty Nolder

New Deal. A grind where you're grinding only on the front truck. Made famous by Neil Blender.

Jolly Mamba. Do a frontside invert (turning the typical 180 degrees). Stall briefly on your hand. Turn an additional 180 degrees and come down the transition fakie.

Elguerial. This challenging stunt was perfected by skating star Eddie Elguera.
1. Go up the transition backward.
2. Grab the board with your lead (backside) hand between your legs on the front rail.
3. Plant your trail (frontside) hand briefly on the coping while pushing off and spinning backside.
4. Spin 360 degrees.
5. Ride down the transition nose first.

Nothing stops the dedicated skater. You bail, wrap a bandage, brandish a grin—and you're off again! Sooner or later, you'll lose any fear of flying. Before you know it, you'll have developed an aerial addiction. Fortunately, if you skate safe, this is one habit that's good for your body and soul.

CONTESTS

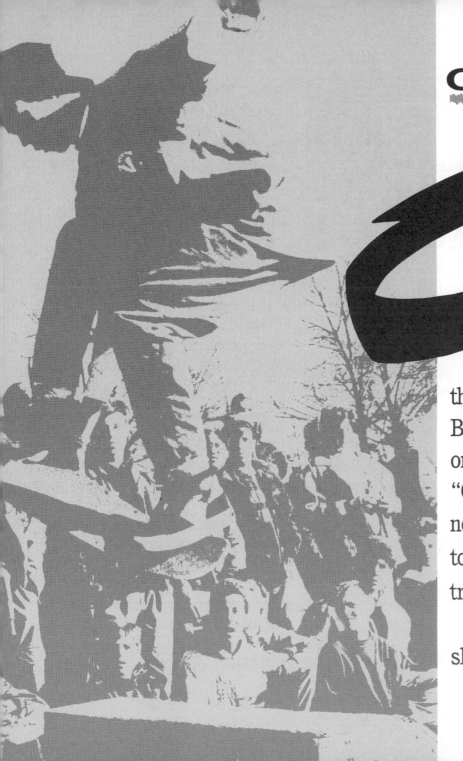

ontests have boosted skateboarding's image as a legitimate sport while giving enthusiasts a chance to see the best skaters in action. You watch, get inspired, and try something new the next time out.

For the pros, contests are part of a career that can earn them $50,000 a year and up. But it goes beyond that. As Stacy Peralta once put it in *Transworld Skateboarding*, "Competition is a gift...no blaring music, no crowd roars, just totally pure concentrated silence."

Contests are about skaters pushing to the

limit—to the realm where body memory disappears and new experience begins. Of course, some fans attend to collect autographs. Others just want the latest stickers. But so what? It doesn't interfere with good skating. Meanwhile, skaters are learning from each other, and the sport advances as a result.

If you're thinking of participating in a national or officially sponsored competition, there are plenty of professional and amateur contests around. Most offer these events:

Freestyle—Individual runs, frequently tied to music. Tricks might include handstand flips, nose wheelies, space walks, spins of all kinds, rail-to-rail flips, pogos, hand flips, and more.

Streetstyle—Skating around, on, and over obstacles such as benches and railroad ties. Usually, there's ramp jumping and wall riding.

Vertical or *Ramp*—The glamor child of skateboarding contests, this event usually features a half-pipe. It's the setting for extensive aerial display and various tricks.

AMATEUR CONTESTS

In the United States, the National Skateboard Association has organized amateur skating into three regions, and each region has two districts. Amateurs must qualify through these contests to be eligible for the national championships, usually held in late December.

Each district contest is limited to 40 skaters. How do you qualify? Through pre-registration, which can be done in a number of ways. You can qualify:

1. Through a local authorized district contest.
2. As a factory team rider.
3. As a shop-sponsored skater.

You become a shop-sponsored skater through word of mouth, by entering contests sponsored by shop owners, or by getting to know retailers in your area. If you want to be sponsored by a manufacturer, you have to be seen by pros and team captains. This means entering lots of contests. You might also try sending a video of yourself skating to a skateboard manufacturer.

Registration information for contests is sent to NSA members six weeks prior to district competitions. Each district contest produces 15 skaters who go on to the regional competition. Of the 30 skaters who compete in each region, ten finalists and two alternates advance to the national championships.

Demonstrating the tricks you've mastered is one reason to enter a contest

Here's how to find your district:

NSA AMATEUR DISTRICTS

EASTERN REGION

Southeast District–Tennessee, North Carolina, South Carolina, Alabama, Georgia, Florida

Northeast District–Virginia, West Virginia, Maryland, Maine, Delaware, District of Columbia, New Jersey, New York, Pennsylvania, Connecticut, Vermont, New Hampshire, Massachusetts

CENTRAL REGION

South Central District–New Mexico, Oklahoma, Texas, Arkansas, Louisiana, Mississippi

North Central District–North Dakota, South Dakota, Nebraska, Iowa, Kansas, Minnesota, Wisconsin, Ohio, Missouri, Illinois, Michigan, Indiana, Kentucky

WESTERN REGION

Southwest District–Southern California, Southern Nevada, Arizona, Hawaii

Northwest District–Washington, Idaho, Montana, Oregon, Utah, Wyoming, Colorado, Northern California, Northern Nevada, Alaska

Kevin Staab pleases the crowd with an aerial

Here's how the districts and regions come together to lead up to the finals.

SOUTHEAST DISTRICT
NORTHEAST DISTRICT . . . . EASTERN REGION . . . . .

NORTH CENTRAL DISTRICT
SOUTH CENTRAL DISTRICT . . . . CENTRAL REGION . . . . FINALS

NORTHWEST DISTRICT
SOUTHWEST DISTRICT . . . . WESTERN REGION . . . . .

Jumping 9½ feet above the coping in San Jose, California, Christian Hosoi set a world record in May, 1988

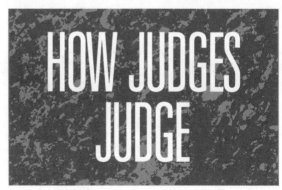

HOW JUDGES JUDGE

Five judges do the scoring at pro contests; amateur competitions usually use three. Judges are expected to know a great deal about skating. They may be skaters, or familiar with the sport through other means such as manufacturing, photography, or coaching.

In vertical skating contests, specific criteria are used in scoring. The composition of the skater's routine or line is considered, as are other aspects, such as: doing as many maneuvers as possible; using all parts of the ramp or area; not wasting set-up walls; and performing to the ultimate limits of the sport without losing control.

Skaters are judged on aggressiveness, difficulty, variety, continuity, originality, and bionics (airs). Although you may be penalized for falls, judges try to take into account how the fall affected your run and the difficulty of the attempted trick.

Freestyle and streetstyle judging use some similar criteria. The tricks themselves count for a great deal, including the number, difficulty, variety, and successful execution. Style counts, too. In freestyle, this means more than just moving in a fluid line—how well your run is choreographed to the music also is important.

LOCAL CONTESTS: HOW TO GET ONE ROLLIN'

Local contests are one of the best ways to build interest in skateboarding—and have fun, too. Contests give skaters a chance to compare, on a competitive level, their individual abilities. Through competitions, local skaters get appreciation and approval from their peers. Contests also often draw skaters from outlying areas who bring in new styles and different tricks. It's a form of cross-pollination.

For a skate shop, the contest creates publicity about the sport and places where skaters can "hang." Contests may be organized by major groups, and your local event can tie-in with a larger group's contest schedule. Bigger associations include the National Skateboarding Association, California Amateur Skateboard League, and the Eastern Skateboarding Association. (See Sources for information about joining associations.)

So you want to get a local contest going, but don't know where to begin? Start with location. Finding a place to hold your competition can be difficult because of insurance liability problems. If someone you know owns a piece of property, or if there's a vacant lot available, you may be home free.

If the property is municipally owned, you must secure permission. You may be

With a little planning, it's easy to organize a contest

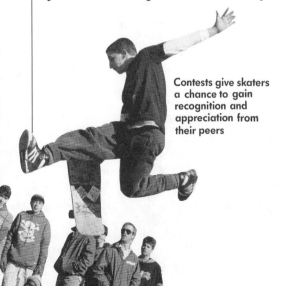
Contests give skaters a chance to gain recognition and appreciation from their peers

required to post a bond as high as $1 million, plus obtain one-day liability insurance. Consult with a local insurance broker for recommendations.

To skirt the issue, skaters sometimes find a gas station or schoolyard and announce a contest. This is fraught with dangers, since the owner may show up and declare the grounds unavailable. Another way to approach the legitimacy issue is to tie into a local charity or service organization such as the Boy Scouts or YMCA. The group's umbrella insurance policy may cover the event and the admission fees will go to charity. This technique opened many skateparks in California.

After you secure a location, go for co-sponsorship. Major manufacturers such

as Vision, Powell-Peralta, Santa Cruz, and others may be willing to help with banners and prizes. They may mail you decks, wheels, or T-shirts, and you can build the event's prestige by using the company's logo in your flyer.

Make a sample flyer and send it to manufacturers at least four to six weeks in advance. Include a cover letter on business stationery with details about the competition: who's entering, local sponsors, contest categories. Ask for any type of help they can give, and be generous with your thanks—both before and after.

The next step is to publicize your contest. Your flyer has to be esthetically attractive to skaters. Use skater-style graphics, but don't make it so cool that you omit the time, date, and place in bold letters. Include a phone number that applicants can call for more information. Send a notice to local newspapers and radio or television stations. If you have the cash, advertise in local skate rags.

Make sure your flyer specifies the registration deadline and any fee. Let applicants know ahead of time what protective gear will be required: for vertical, knee pads, elbow pads, and helmets are a must; for street, protective gear isn't mandatory, but it sure doesn't hurt. If rules and regs are clear well in advance of the competition, it really cuts down on a lot of groaning and moaning from skaters who weren't aware of the requirements.

If you're expecting a large turnout, pre-register contestants about ten days before the event. Try to limit the total time of the contest—four hours seems to be the upper limit. Figure out how much time you can allow for each skater to determine how many you can register. For example, if the contest's going to run 240 minutes, you have to subtract time for each skater's run (one minute) and time for judges' breaks (five to ten minutes after each division). Then decide

how many skaters will be allowed to compete in each category.

How do you establish categories? Any way you prefer. Here is a simple breakdown for a street and freestyle contest:

1. 13 and under
2. 14 to 16
3. 17 and over
4. amateurs sponsored by shops or companies
5. freestyle (Freestyle usually has fewer entrants because it requires specialization.)

Many contest organizers also have skaters sign liability waivers at pre-registration. These may not stand up in court if a skater is injured, but they might discourage lawsuits.

Music and food are two other details that should be handled early. At NSA contests, runs are choreographed to music. At the local level, settle for skate rock tapes. Ask the contestants about their preferences. Line up the tapes and rent or borrow a quality sound system. Even better is a live band for a jam after the contest.

Tell vendors well in advance so you can be sure of sufficient food. Have running water on hand or bring bottled

mineral water for the contestants.

Now you're rollin'. Secure the wood or other obstacles you need for a streetstyle contest. Lately, obstacles have been getting wilder—snakelike lengths of pipe and plywood twisted into virtual roller coasters for slitherin' sliders.

Build a street ramp or an actual rail slide. A rail slide can be fashioned from a single piece of 6″ diameter PVC pipe. It has to be firmly secured in the ground with stakes or nails. Get about six to eight feet of pipe, and put a 2″ × 4″ through the length of it. Attach 4″ × 4″ wooden blocks to the end to get the rail up off of the ground.

Another common obstacle is the vertical wall. Put a street ramp next to it for combination runs. One option is to have one vertical wall on its own and a second that's near a quarter-pipe ramp. An ollie box creates another twist in street style. It's a huge wooden box, 2′ × 5′ × 5′, with

The 'truckstand' is a spectator trick

coping around the corners so you can slide or grind off all the edges.

Maybe your local auto shop will donate a wreck for tricks. (If it's not a wreck now, it will be when the contest's finished!) Put a ramp up to the car and see if you can do 540s over it, skate down the fenders, ollie airs, and anything else skaters devise. The resulting spectacle is "sort of like Evel Knievel in bizarro world," according to Richard Roberts of Spike's Skates in Philadelphia.

Once the obstacles are nailed down (sometimes literally), it's time to line up judges. They should know a great deal about the sport, and should not be contestants themselves. This last requirement can put a crimp in your recruiting since people who know skating usually are skaters.

Offer your judges some form of compensation—shirts, lunch, stickers, *something* to make it worthwhile. Get the best judges available; ones who know the difference between flash and true technique. They also should not be biased in favor of their friends or influenced by crowd reaction—how loud people clap and shout may have nothing to do with the difficulty of a run. A skater should be judged against other contestants—not against a previous performance or his reputation.

Don't penalize people too much for falling—it discourages them from trying new tricks. Anyway, a contestant who falls may have been trying a much harder trick than one who made a flawless run.

Provide the judges with scoring sheets. List the tricks and provide space for the judges to write in a score from 1 to 10 for each trick.

Here's a sample scoring sheet you might use:

PHILLY FREEZE SCORE SHEET!

JUDGE'S NAME		
NAME	NAME	NAME
INVTS	INVTS	INVTS
AIRS	AIRS	AIRS
OLLIES	OLLIES	OLLIES
WALLS	WALLS	WALLS
SLIDES/STRT	SLIDES/STREET	SLIDES/STRT
STYLE	STYLE	STYLE
MISC!	MISC!	MISC!
TOTAL	TOTAL	TOTAL
NAME	NAME	NAME
INVTS	INVTS	INVTS
AIRS	AIRS	AIRS
OLLIES	OLLIES	OLLIES
WALLS	WALLS	WALLS
SLIDES/STRT	SLIDES/STRT	SLIDES/STRT
STYLE	STYLE	STYLE
MISC!	MISC!	MISC!
TOTAL	TOTAL	TOTAL
NAME	NAME	NAME
INVTS	INVTS	INVTS
AIRS	AIRS	AIRS
OLLIES	OLLIES	OLLIES
WALLS	WALLS	WALLS
SLIDES/STREET	SLIDES/STRT	SLIDES/STRT
STYLE	STYLE	STYLE
MISC!	MISC!	MISC!
TOTAL	TOTAL	TOTAL

At the end of the runs in each division, add up the total number of points for each skater and divide by the number of judges. Thus you arrive at first, second, and third place, and honorable mention. The averaging process helps you attain consistency in judging.

After each division, announce the five finalists. They can stay to compete—either immediately or later in the day. The others can then leave if they want to. Build suspense by waiting until the end of the day to announce winners in all categories.

Prizes should be of equal value since the best skaters in each division compete at their own level. Skate equipment and accessories, cash, or trophies are great prizes.

After the competition, you or the most admired skater should ask everyone to "pick up one soda can." Responsibility for cleaning up trash rests ultimately with the sponsor. The local reputation of skateboarding will depend in part on what the site looks like when you leave.

When the contest's over, you'll have had plenty of fun...and loads of memories to cherish.

BUILDING RAMPS & WALLS

You're a hot skater. You've shredded local streets 'til you know every bump, curve, and rail worth riding. And still you have a taste for more. So what are you waiting for? Now's the time to give yourself some air—thrasher-style.

This chapter contains basic instructions on how to build a rideable wall and three kinds of ramps: a launch ramp, a quarter-pipe, and a half-pipe.

Before you grab a hammer and nails, here's some advice about location: never put ramps in the street. Find yourself a nice piece of vacant land, or even a seldom-used sidewalk, for a vertical ramp. Traffic and launch ramps just don't mix. Half-pipes seem to find good homes in back yards, although a more public place is ideal so you won't disturb the neighbors.

All of these projects can be built using standard tools: a circular saw for vertical cuts; a saber saw for notches; a power drill; a hammer and a screwdriver (invest in a power screwdriver if you're using lots of screws). Be extra cautious when using power tools and wear safety goggles to protect your eyes.

These ramps will last longer and serve you well if you prime and protect the wood. Outdoor urethane is expensive (a gallon can add $20 to your construction costs) but it's worth it if you want your ramp to last. If urethane busts your budget, coat the ramp or wall with wood primer and outdoor paint.

Now let's get started; simpler things first...

A simple launch ramp gets John Thomas goin'

THE LAUNCH RAMP

This kind of ramp, also called a jump ramp, will help you get airborne. With practice, you'll find yourself using it for airs, 180s, 360s, and much more. If you build it with handholes, your ramp will be completely portable.

The basic materials for a launch ramp are:
- Four 4′ × 8′ sheets of ⅝″ plywood
- One 4′ × 8′ sheet of ⅜″ plywood
- One 4′ × 8′ sheet of ⅛″ plywood
- One piece of plywood cut 8″ × 4′
- Nine sections of 2 × 4 cut in 3′ 10¾″ lengths
- Two lengths of 2 × 4 about 8′ long
- Nails and wood screws

Approximate cost: $45

This plan creates a launch ramp that's 4′ wide, 36″ high, and has an 8″-wide top deck.

Step 1. Draw cutting guidelines for the exterior templates of ⅝″ plywood. Begin with one 4′ × 8′ sheet of plywood. Draw a dotted line 36″ from the bottom across the long side of the plywood (figure 1).

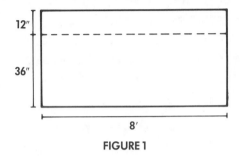

FIGURE 1

To create your riding slope, draw a 9′ radius to define the arc, or curve, of the ramp. Place a 9′ length of 2 × 4 (or get someone to help you hold taut a 9′ length of string) at the narrow end of the plywood sheet. Attach a pencil or marker to the bottom of the 2 × 4. At the other end of the 2 × 4, which will be the axis or stationary point, secure it by driving a long nail through the lumber and into the ground (unless, of course, you're in the garage!). Now swing your 2 × 4 to mark a curved line leading up to the 36″ high dotted line (figure 2).

Define the top deck by marking 8″ along the dotted line past the intersection of the arc. From that point, draw a line straight down to the bottom of the plywood (figure 3). Now you've defined the basic shape of your templates. The angle you have created is crucial to giving you thrust without sending you straight up into the air or slithering over the edge.

Cut out this piece and use it as a guideline to cut three more templates from 4′ × 8′ sheets of ⅝″ plywood.

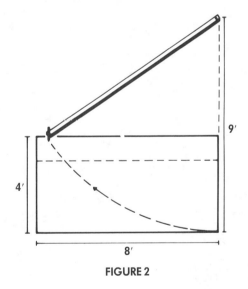

FIGURE 2

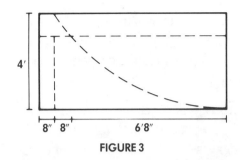

FIGURE 3

Step 2. Take two templates and cut off 6″ from the narrowest portion at the bottom. These will become the interior templates. Set aside the other two for the exterior.

Mark and cut notches 4″ wide and 2″ deep near the top and bottom of your curve, another at the back of the top deck, and a fourth at the back, along the bottom. Along the riding slope, mark and cut five evenly spaced notches 2″ wide and 4″ deep. These will allow you to nail in 2 × 4 crosspiece ribs for interior support (figure 4).

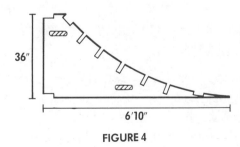

FIGURE 4

If you plan on handholes, mark and cut them on all four templates before joining the interior and exterior templates.

Step 3. Nail or screw two templates (one interior, one exterior) together to make a joined set. These sets are mirror opposites, so the notched templates must face inward (figure 5).

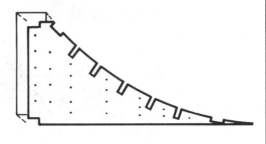

FIGURE 5

Step 4. Cut nine lengths of 2 × 4, each 3′ 10¾″ long. (I've subtracted a half-inch on each end to account for the flush exterior plywood.) If you use ½″ plywood for templates, be sure to compensate the 2 × 4 lengths.

Step 5. Join the 2 × 4 crosspieces to your templates by driving nails or by fastening screws through the exterior plywood template into the 2 × 4 ends (figure 6).

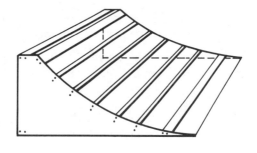

FIGURE 6

Add diagonal nails or screws for additional strength. Join the bottom and top rear 2 × 4 supports with nails or screws.

Step 6. For side-to-side support, add two diagonal 2 × 4 braces to the inside of the boxy end of the ramp. If you're a talented carpenter, these can be cut at their ends so that they lie flush. If not, at least nail the butt edges of the boards in place at the juncture of the other 2 × 4s. Cut a board 8″ × 4′ for your top deck and nail or screw it down (figure 7). (You should have plenty of scrap left from building the templates.)

Step 7. Apply the top layers of plywood. Find the length of riding surface by lay-

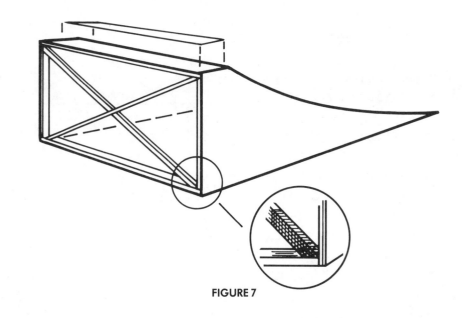

FIGURE 7

ing a tape measure along the curved edge of the plywood template. Then measure and cut the ⅜″ plywood sheet.

Begin applying the riding surface at the top and work your way down, nailing into the ribs as well as the edges (figure 8). Countersink the screwheads and counterpunch the nailheads. Repeat the process with the ¼″ plywood sheet.

Step 8. Coat with outdoor urethane and launch!

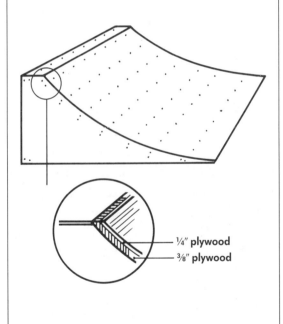

¼″ plywood
⅜″ plywood

FIGURE 8

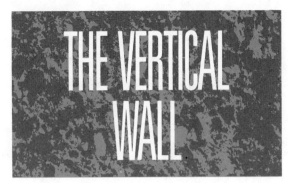

THE VERTICAL WALL

Sometimes, the urban or suburban landscape won't cooperate in your quest for the perfect challenge. In a sea of walls, none is available for skaters. "Too much noise" and "Go do it in your own back yard, kid," are common kinds of static.

Fortunately, building a vertical wall is one of the easiest of skate carpentry challenges. Essentially, you're creating an 8′ × 8′ square of wall for riding. It should be straight and sturdy; you may want to place a quarter-pipe up against it for more fun.

The basic materials for a rideable wall are:

- Two 4′ × 8′ sheets of ⅜″ plywood
- Four 8′ lengths of 2 × 4
- One 9′ length of 2 × 4
- Two 2 × 4s at least 10½′ long

Mike Garcia combines a launch ramp and vertical wall for skate thrills

- Nails
- Two heavy spikes or pegs
- Sand bags or concrete blocks

Approximate cost: $45

Step 1. Frame two 4′ × 8′ plywood sheets with 2 × 4 to create a large, sturdy square. Nail all the 2 × 4s through the 4″ sides (except along the bottom of the wall, which uses the 9′ timber). Always nail from the plywood side through to the 2 × 4. Nail one 2 × 4 down the middle seam to prevent separation. On the bottom, nail through the 2″ side of the 2 × 4, which should be about 6″ longer on either side to hold support spikes (figure 9).

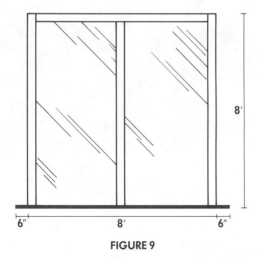

FIGURE 9

Step 2. If you're going to put your wall in the dirt—at the edge of a sidewalk or driveway—drill diagonal holes in the bottom protruding 2 × 4 and drive long, heavy nails, spikes, or pegs through to brace the wall at the bottom whenever you're riding (figure 10).

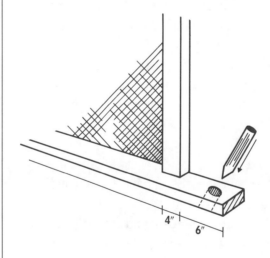

FIGURE 10

If you're placing your wall on pavement, stack sand bags or concrete blocks on the protruding 2 × 4 for support.

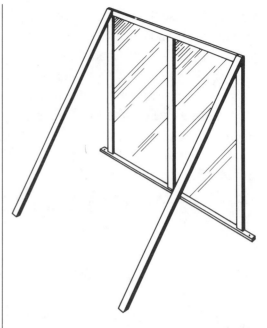

FIGURE 11

Step 3. Run diagonal 2 × 4s from the top corners to the ground behind the wall (figure 11). Use thick wood screws at the top so you'll be able to dismantle the wall. The diagonal supports should be at least 10½′ long, but can be even longer if you plan to bury them in the ground. Work the 2 × 4 supports into the dirt, or brace them against a curb or other immoveable object.

Step 4. Coat with outdoor urethane or paint. Result: A pleasure wall for skaters.

THE QUARTER-PIPE

There are all kinds of pipe dreams, but skaters are lucky enough to have their dreams come true on quarter-pipes and half-pipes. A quarter-pipe looks like its name, and its main function is to help you skate vertical. A quarter-pipe with a high, wide radius can be used for many of the same tricks you'd attempt on a half-pipe, such as airs or inverts. The plans for the quarter-pipe below are on the small side in radius—4 feet—but that makes it pretty portable and well-suited for streetstyle antics.

Build two of these babies and place them side by side in front of your vertical wall. Then try turning frontside or backside, going vert, and coming down nose first, instead of fakie. If you want a quarter-pipe with a bigger radius, adapt the plans for the template method half-pipe later in this chapter.

This quarter pipe has no roll-out deck. It's for vertical wall riding. Don't use it as a jump ramp or you'll bail pretty bad.

The basic materials for a quarter-pipe are:
- One 4 × 8 sheet of ½″ or ⅝″ plywood
- 10 sections of 2 × 4 cut into 4′ lengths
- Two sections of 2 × 4 cut into 5¾′ lengths
- Two 4 × 8 sheets of ¼″ plywood
- Nails

Approximate cost: $45

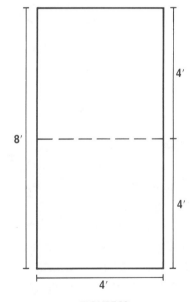

FIGURE 12

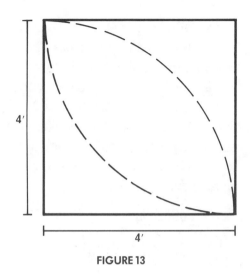

FIGURE 13

Step 1. Cut the 4 × 8 sheet of ½″ or ⅝″ plywood into two 4 × 4 squares (figure 12).

Step 2. Drive a nail into one of the upper corners. Take a 4′ long string, tie a pencil to one end and tie the other end to the nail. Holding the string taut, draw an arc as you guide the pencil down to the opposite corner. Move the nail to the opposite corner and mark another template (figure 13); then mark your final template on the second 4 × 4 square. Cut out three templates.

Step 3. Select one template to be the interior template. Mark notches 4″ wide and 2″ deep near the top and bottom of the arc, and at the back top and bottom of the template. Mark six notches 2″ wide and 4″ deep at 6″ intervals on the curve between the larger notches at the top and bottom (figure 14). Cut notches with a saber and circular saw.

Step 4. Cut handholes into ends of both exterior templates. Drill a pilot hole and then cut with a saber saw.

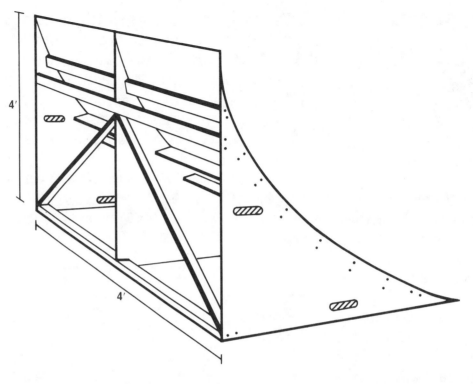

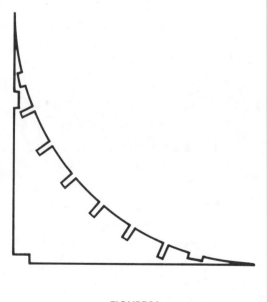

FIGURE 14

Step 5. Nail the exterior templates to the ends of the 4′ lengths of 2 × 4, which should fit snugly into the notches cut into the interior template. Nail the top and bottom 2 × 4s first, then fill in the curve (as in figure 6). Hammer nails on the diagonal. Reinforce the back of the quarter-pipe with two diagonal supports (figure 15).

Step 6. Apply the skating surface. Nail a 4 × 8 sheet of ¼″ plywood into every 2 × 4. Cut off the excess board at the bottom. Then apply a second layer of ¼″ ply and cut at the bottom, making sure you meet the ground (figure 16). Taper the bottom edge so it touches the ground evenly—you don't want to hit that ply and go flying.

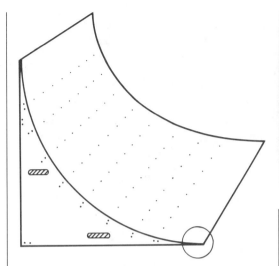

FIGURE 16

Step 7. Coat with outdoor urethane. Carry it to a wall and let the fun begin!

A transition is like a booster rocket—it gets you up where you want to be

THE HALF-PIPE

If you're serious about skating vert, there's nothing that compares with a half-pipe. Other plans in this chapter call for a

minimum investment of time and space. This one is for the dedicated thrasher—and half a dozen friends—because it's big, maybe even too big for the back yard. But what a great ramp training ground!

Here are the awesome dimensions: 9′ of transition; 1½′ of vert; 16′ of flat; 16′ wide; and a 4′ roll-out deck at each end. With this kind of width, you'll have plenty of space for full airs without worrying about missing the edge of the ramp, or having to ride back fakie the way you might with narrower half-pipes.

A half-pipe of this size really isn't portable, so when you're selecting a site, remember the old real estate saying about the three most important considerations in buying a new home: location, location, and location. You don't want to spend a grand or so of your hard-earned cash, plus umpteen hours of labor, just to have your mom condemn it as an eyesore, or have the neighbors complain that it's a public nuisance. So as I said at the beginning of this chapter, scope out the situation from all angles. When the signals are GO, you and your skate carpenter pals should be stoked for your biggest challenge yet—a little Cape Canaveral of your own.

The approximate materials for this half-pipe are:

- 100 4′ × 8′ sheets of ⅜″ CDX plywood for surfacing and internal and external templates
- 56 4 × 4 timbers 4′ long for the base frame (get rounded timbers like those used in gardening)
- 70 16′ lengths of 2 × 4 for crossbeams and internal bracing
- 16′ of PVC pipe, cut in half lengthwise
- Screws or nails (nails are recommended for ease of assembly; screws if you think you'll have to dismantle your ramp)

Approximate cost: $800 to $1,200

This design has no channel or roll-in since the gap in the coping can impede your lip work. With practice, you'll get used to dropping from the roll-out deck.

Step 1. Create a rectangular frame. The whole ramp rests on this substructure, so make it level and strong. Build a giant rectangle—42′ long, 16′ 4″ wide—out of 4 × 4 timbers (or if absolutely necessary, 2 × 4s). Join the timbers by nailing into them diagonally along the sides (figure 17).

Check all the way around with a carpenter's level to be sure the structure is completely flat. If you're building on dirt, dig out high areas and build up low ones; on asphalt, build up low areas with wood supports.

Step 2. Build a support structure within the frame. Run a full length of timbers down the middle of the 42′ length of the rectangle, nailing in the same manner as with the outer frame. Inside the framework, create support "boxes" with 2 × 4s for the roll-out decks, and vertical and transitional areas. Measure 2′ from the end of the frame and nail a line of timbers across the width of the frame (16′ 4″). Measure 11′ from that line and nail another line of timbers across. Divide each area into four subsections and reinforce with diagonal supports (figure 18). You now have three internal and two external areas to support the templates.

Nail the same internal framework into the other end of the rectangle.

Step 3. Build the templates. You'll need 10 of them; six will become interior templates and four exterior templates.

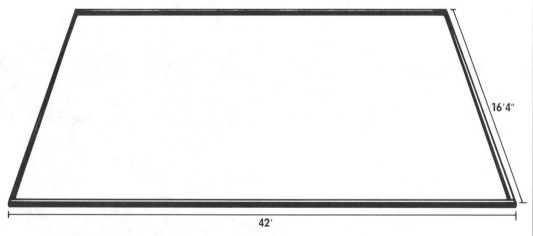

16′4″

42′

FIGURE 17

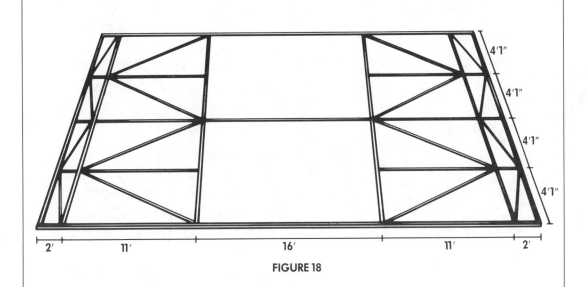

FIGURE 18

2' 11' 16' 11' 2'

4'1"
4'1"
4'1"
4'1"

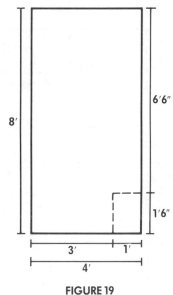

FIGURE 19

8'
6'6"
1'6"
3'
1'
4'

First, cut a rectangular inset 1½' long and 1' wide into one 4' × 8' sheet of ⅝" plywood (figure 19). Lay two sheets of plywood together as shown, with the corner of one fitting into the inset of the other (figure 20).

Use a 2 × 4 a little over 9' long to mark the radius of the transitions. Drive a heavy nail into one end (for a pivot) and attach a pencil or marker to the other end so that the distance between the points is exactly 9'. (You can do the same with a string held taut.) Measure 3⅜"

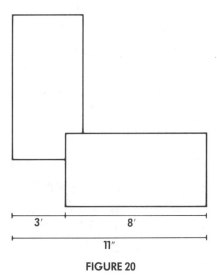

FIGURE 20

3' 8'
11"

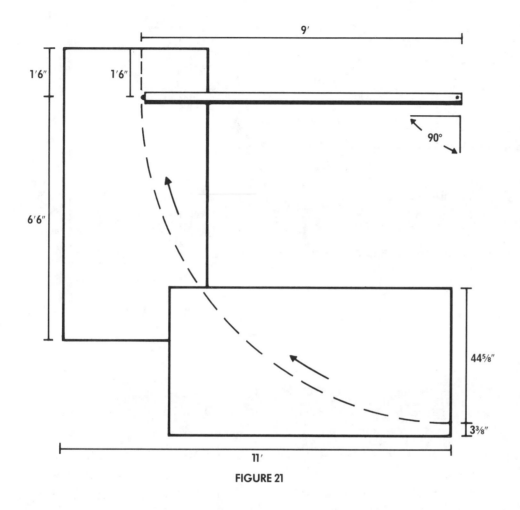

9'

1'6"

1'6"

6'6"

90°

44⅝"

3⅜"

11'

FIGURE 21

vertical rise straight up to the top (figure 21). Now cut the lines you've marked. These are your master sections.

Use these masters to create nine more templates. Use pieces of plywood scrap to bridge the two template sections, thus forming a complete template.

Step 4. Notch six templates so that they can accept resting crossbeams. These will be your interior templates. Mark and cut four notches 4" wide and 2" deep along the bottom of the arc; then cut notches 2" wide and 4" deep up the rest of the arc until you reach the vert area. Space the notches 4" to 6" apart on the transition; 8" apart on the vert (figure 22).

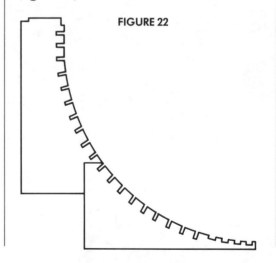

FIGURE 22

from the lower corner of the bottom board and make a mark. This point is the end of your radius, and where the pencil or marker should rest. The stationary point (axis) of the radius is 9' straight up along the edge of the lower plywood section. Swing the 2 × 4 so that it creates a clear mark in a circular arc, stopping 1½' before the top of the second piece of plywood. From that point, mark 1½' of

Many thrashers can only dream about skating ramps like this beauty below Kevin Staab

Starting at the top of the template, make sure there's a notch every 4' along the entire length of the ramp. This spacing is important because you'll be nailing the plywood surface into the 2 × 4s below.

Step 5. Nail a 2 × 4 along the outside bottom of one exterior template, and another running vertically along the inside of the upright spine. Place a scrap piece of plywood at the juncture of the two 2 × 4 reinforcements, so you can nail through them to make a solid joint (figure 23). Do the same with a second exterior template, but remember to make it a mirror opposite of the first. Then build another set for the opposite end of the half-pipe.

Interior templates can have 2 × 4 reinforcements running along any edge, if you want to add them. Repeat the entire process to create six interior templates.

All finished? Pat yourself on the back! This is one of the hardest parts of building your ramp.

Step 6. Raise your templates. Like a barn raising, you'll want to whip up some community spirit when it's time to put the templates in place. Get a bunch of

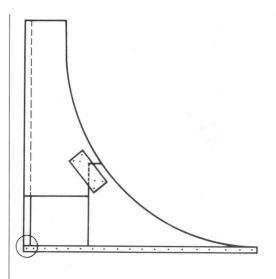

FIGURE 23

skaters together to help you raise and nail them into place.

Before placing your templates upright, make sure there's exactly 16' of "flatland" between transitions. This ensures that the plywood surface—in 8' lengths—will be nailed into something other than air. Locate the mid-point of your ramp's bottom framework; then measure 8' in both directions to mark the bottom point of your transitions.

Now you're ready to line up the first set of exterior templates. Temporarily nail a 16' 2 × 4 behind them to line them up. Now lift them and nail them into the timbers at the bottom of the frame. This creates a kind of box to hold the interior templates (figure 24).

Insert the interior templates and butt them against the temporary 2 × 4. Make sure everything is flush and level. When you're certain, nail permanent cross-pieces of 2 × 4 to make sure the structure doesn't move (figure 25). Repeat the same process at the opposite end of the ramp.

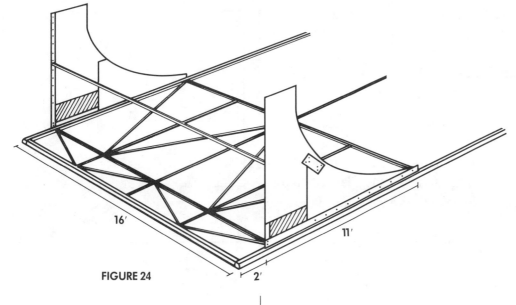

16'

11'

2'

FIGURE 24

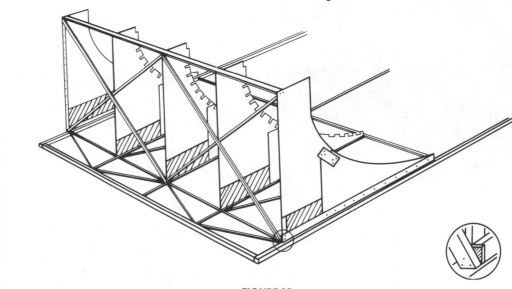

FIGURE 25

Step 7. Prepare the flat area, or "flatland." The crossbeams in the flat need to rest on something. Remember that your transitional surface will end up 3⅜" above the top of the flatland timbers.

Now create a "lip" of 2 × 4s (narrow side up) along the wide edge of the exterior timbers of the flat. These will form a box to hold the 16' 2 × 4 support beams. Nail the 2 × 4s directly into the timber–making sure you allow 16' of width from one inner edge to the other (figure 26).

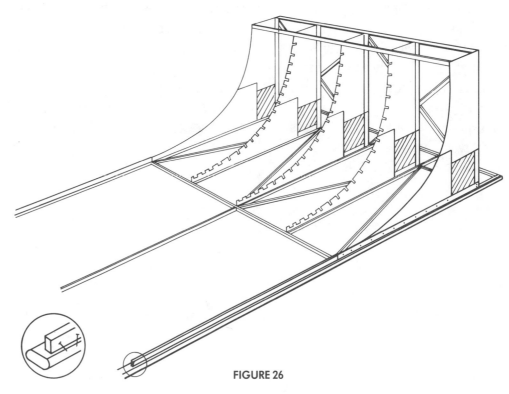

FIGURE 26

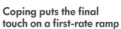

Coping puts the final touch on a first-rate ramp

Step 8. After completing the box, fill it with 16′ long crossbeams, with the 2″ side facing up. Space them about 12″ apart in the flat. The plywood surface is nailed directly to these stubby, but important, supports.

Install the transition template crossbeams, which are what the surface rests upon. Nail the butts of your 16′ lengths into the exterior templates and notches using 8p or 10p common nails (figure 27). The level of the lowest 2 × 4 support at the bottom of the transition template should be the same as the level of the last 2 × 4 at the end of your flat, thus creating a perfect line from curve to flat.

Erik Castro enjoys a backyard ramp session

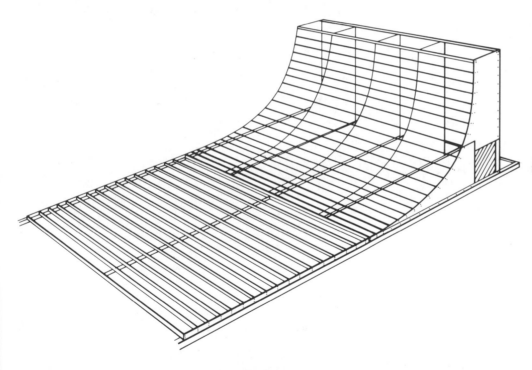

FIGURE 27

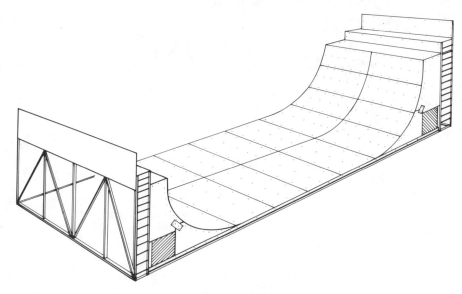

FIGURE 28

Step 9. Apply the surface. Use one layer of ⅜″ CDX plywood and ring or grip nails, since there's a lot of structural pressure trying to pull up the plywood.

Drive in nails every 6″ across the narrow ends of the plywood sheets and into every 2 × 4 going across the flat, transition, and vert. Space nails every 2″ along all seams.

To find underlying 2 × 4s, team up with a friend to use a chalk snap line from both ends. This will make it easy to drive nails into the 2 × 4 rather than air! A snap line can be bought in most hard-ware stores. Run it along the area you want to mark. With one person on each side of the ramp, center the line above the 2 × 4 (you can see the butt end through the template). Now snap the line and you've got it chalked across the ramp.

Add a second layer of ⅜″ CDX plywood surface.

Step 10. Build the roll-out decks and ladders. This plan calls for spacious roll-out decks to accommodate the mobs of friends you'll suddenly make. Use ply-wood and 2 × 4s to fill in the top and make your buddies comfortable on a bench about 2′ high with a 4′ high back support (figure 28). Buy a ladder to attach to the side, or build one with rungs spaced about a foot apart.

Step 9. Install coping. Use 2″ diameter PVC pipe for a good, slippery coping. Cut it in half lengthwise with a circular or band saw. Then drill holes in it, counter-sink the holes with a countersink drill, and install coping across the top lips of your ramp.

Step 10. Protect your masterpiece with outdoor urethane. It's expensive, but worth it. Use several extra coats at the bottoms of the transitions, where abuse is most severe.

If you live where there's snow or ice in winter, protect your ramp with heavy mil plastic weighted with bricks or taped down with duct tape.

Congratulations—You've passed your apprenticeship in skate carpentry. Now it's time to fly!

REFLECTIONS

CHAPTER 8

hink about the planet. One-fourth of it is land mass. And a good part of that is interlaced with paved surfaces...ready for you to explore via skateboard. What's out there? The possibilities abound.

Empty pools in Tel Aviv...causeways through the Amazonian jungle...Casablanca alleys (Skate it again, Sam)...the Great Wall of China...the Kona ramp in Hawaii...twists and turns in the Burma Road...the fountain plaza at Lincoln Center... the terraces of the Sydney Opera House...the copings of Copenhagen.

The skater keeps a steady hand on the horizon, even when the whole world is spinning

Or anywhere a skater puts urethane to asphalt.

Skateboarding has had its ups and downs, but nobody will ever put a spike through this sport's heart. Just can't happen. Skating has too much going for it. The boards are so good, the territory so available, the air so free, and the ramps so easy to build.

Skating, in the final analysis, is in the blood. If you've got skating in you, it must come to the surface. Maybe it's because polyurethane is an organic compound and, like paint thinner, it penetrates deeply into human tissue.

Whatever the reason, even if you abandon skateboarding, it won't abandon you. In some distant decade, you may meet a new generation of thrashers and

decide to get back on your board. Body memory will take over and a hidden program booted two decades ago will kick in. Then you'll find your middle-aged frame doing Smith grinds and layback rollouts!

Maybe you'll teach airs and ollies to your kids. Even if skating isn't hot in the 21st century, you'll probably get them boards anyway. Parents will always give their children the things that they most loved as children.

And don't be surprised when the kiddies spacewalk to Neptune to try out some really rad craters. Or baffle you with the Black Hole boneless and UFO railslide. Hey, that's just the tip of the flaming action ahead.

So keep rippin.'

The dedicated thrasher skates anytime, anywhere

ASSOCIATIONS

PUBLICATIONS

sticker. This group, for skaters east of the Mississippi, organizes amateur competitions and sets uniform judging standards.

National Skateboard Association
P.O. Box 3645
San Bernadino, CA 92413
(714) 882-3406

Membership is $20 a year, and entitles you to a T-shirt, membership card, information booklet, decals, newsletters, and discounts at NSA events.

Regional Associations

California Amateur Skateboard League
P.O. Box 3004
San Bernadino, CA 92413

Eastern Skateboarding Association
101 Warren Avenue
Seekonk, MA 02771
(617) 336-9563

A membership fee of $12 covers membership card, T-shirt, newsletter, and

ELECTRONIC BULLETIN BOARD

THRASHER BBS (Bulletin Board System)
(415) 822-5630

Hook up your computer to this line via modem and get the latest contest results, news, exchange messages, and more.

Thrasher
High Speed Productions, Inc.
P.O. Box 884570
San Francisco, CA 94188-4570
(415) 822-3083

Thrasher magazine, a national monthly, is available by subscription for $12 per year.

Transworld Skateboarding
Imprimatur, Inc.
353 Airport Road
Oceanside, CA 92054

Subscriptions to this national monthly magazine are $14 per year.

Regional 'Zines

Bow to No Man
Box 2433
Scottsdale, AZ 85252

Gut Feel'n
5130 Kaiser Avenue
Santa Barbara, CA 93111

Hick Town
Route 3, Box 233
Idaho Falls, ID 83401

Killer Dork Sessions
11409 Daisy Lane
Glenn Dale, MD 20769

100% Funzine
4221 Mill Stream Court
Virginia Beach, VA 23542

Rat Bite
18 High Pool Close
Newton, Swansea SA34TV
United Kingdom

Skate Threat
566 Northlawn Court
Lancaster, PA 15213

VIDEOS

Look for some of the following titles at your local video rental store. Watch selected scenes in slow motion to get a good feel for how the pros handle the toughest tricks. Most videos are produced by manufacturers.

National Skateboarding Association contest videos: *Southwest Regional Championships; Down South at the Ranch; Eastern Assault; Oceanside Street Attack; Chicago Blowout.*

Powell-Peralta: *The Bones Brigade; Future Primitive; The Search for Animal Chin.*

Santa Cruz: *Wheels of Fire.*
Gullwing: *Molecules in Motion.*
Vision: *Skatevisions.*

RAMP PLANS

CAD/D Applications
P.O. Box 5579, Dept. TW
Albuquerque, NM 87185
  Computer-generated plans, including instructions and materials list.

Rampage Designs
P.O. Box 1464
Springfield, OR 97477
  Plans for a street ramp in ten easy steps.

MANUFACTURERS

LEGEND:

 = accessories
(grip tape, risers, etc.)

 = decks

 = skateboards

 = shoes

 = sportswear

 = trucks

 = protective wear

 = wheels

 = videos

 = stickers

A Skater's Paradise
537 State Street
Santa Barbara, CA 93101
(805) 962-2526
 Offers advice on setting up public jam sessions/contests. If you have questions, just send a self-addressed, stamped envelope.

Action Sports Skateboards
3260 Pomona Boulevard
Pomona, CA 91768

Airwalk
Department Th-3
P.O. Box 9000-227
Carlsbad, CA 92009

Alva
32991 Calle Aviador-F
San Juan Capistrano, CA 92675
 Alva produces a complete pro line of skateboards and accessories.

Baddboys
P.O. Box 40727
Santa Barbara, CA 93101
(805) 683-1236
 Offers bare decks in various shapes and sizes, including un-cut (Create-A-Skate). Also unassembled complete board kits, including epoxy decks.

Bare Cover
1312 West Southern Avenue
Mesa, AZ 85202
 Carries a broad range of skate shoes.

Blockhead Skates
102 Lincoln Street
Roseville, CA 95678
(916) 782-2102

Brand X
4693-4 Telephone Road #120
Ventura, CA 93003

CAD/D Applications
P.O. Box 5579, Dept. TW
Albuquerque, NM 87185
   Makes computer generated ramp
plans for street, wave, quarter pipes,
half-pipes, and other types.

Cal Skate & Sport
213 Northwest Couch Street
Portland, OR 97209
1 (800) 44-SKATE

California Cheap Skates
986 Monterey Street
San Luis Obispo, CA 93401

California Hot Products
2511-P
West La Palma Avenue
Anaheim, CA 92801
1 (800) HOT-3233
In California: 1 (800) 4CALHOT
   Complete skateboards as low as
$39.95.

California Skate Express
5054 North Blackstone, Suite 105
Fresno, CA 93710
1 (800) 447-8989 (Orders Only)
(209) 229-7171
   A complete mail order house.

California Streets
11 Lonsdale
North Vancouver, B.C.
Canada V7M 2E4
(604) 984-8559

California Surf Style
986 Monterey Street, Dept. 3
San Luis Obispo, CA 93401
1 (800) 843-1336
In California: (805) 543-0597

D-Wing Skates
P.O. Box 831
College Park, MD 20740
1 (800) 44D-WING
   Can special order a variety of decks.

Deluxe
P.O. Box 883311
San Francisco, CA 94188

Dogtown Skates
P.O. Box 5512
Venice, CA 90296

Eastern Skateboard Supply
702 North West Street
Raleigh, NC 27603
   Distributors of several national brands
of skateboards and accessories.

FTC Skate & Surf
1586 Bush at Franklin
San Francisco, CA 94109
(415) 673-8361

Go Skate!
150A Gilman Avenue
Campbell, CA 95008
(408) 866-2244

Gotcha Sportswear, Inc.
P.O. Box 5024
Costa Mesa, CA 92628

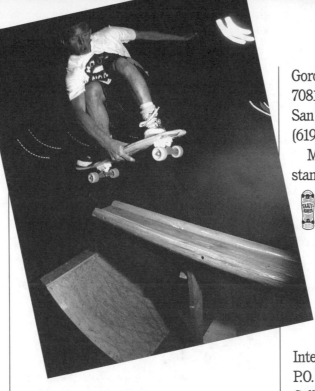

Gremic
15679 Los Gatos Boulevard
Los Gatos, CA 95030
(408) 358-1169

Gullwing Products
1112 Pioneer Way
El Cajon, CA 92020

Gordon & Smith
7081 Consolidated Way
San Diego, CA 92121-2604
(619) 549-2690
   Makes Nicky Guerrero boards,
standard & mini.

Intensity Skates
P.O. Box 1037
College Park, MD 20740
(301) 345-2252
   Has a full line of brand name boards
and accessories.

J & D Athletic Supply
1040 Northeast Sixteenth Street
Ocala, FL 32670
1 (800) 423-8733 or (800) 423-7408
   Wholesale to the trade only.

JFA Skateboards
Placebo Products
P.O. Box 23316
Phoenix, AZ 85063

Jimmy' Z
1809 Hardeman Avenue
Macon, GA 31202
Orders only: 1 (800) 222-5615
Questions & service: (912) 746-3761

Kryptonics
5660 Central Avenue
Boulder, CO 80301
(303) 442-9173

Lake Skates
7800 Industrial Street
West Melbourne, FL 32901
(301) 951-8160

Madrid Skateboards
P.O. Box 2845
Santa Fe Springs, CA 90670
(213) 946-9918

Motobilt
19803 Almaden Road
San Jose, CA 95120

Mr. Wilson's Skateboards
P.O. Box 902
Neenah, WI 54956

NSI Video
P.O. Box 895
Hermosa Beach, CA 90254

Naked Boards
P.O. Box 149
Wittman, MD 21676
(301) 745-2187 (Baltimore, MD)
(303) 449-8006 (Boulder, CO)
   Minis and uncut boards.

Nash Manufacturing, Inc.
315 West Ripy
Forth Worth, TX 76110
1 (800) 433-2901
In Texas: (817) 926-5223
   Nash makes a tiny board—15" long—
that fits into most school lockers.

Ocean Avenue
Total Skateboard Distribution
P.O. Box 1331
Cocoa Beach, FL
(305) 799-2158
   This is a distribution company for dealers only. Handles many major brands.

Orange Cycle Decks
2204 Edgewater Drive
Orlando, FL 32804
Orders only: 1 (800) 423-9805
Questions: (305) 841-2484
   Carries decks, hundreds of buttons, and saw blades.

Palo Alto Sport Shop
526 Waverly Street
Palo Alto, CA 94301
(415) 328-8556

Powell Peralta
501 East Gutierrez Street
Santa Barbara, CA 93103
(805) 963-0416

Pro-Designed Knee Pads
P.O. Box 925213
Houston, TX 77292
(718) 957-0341
   Makes a wide variety of knee pads in various sizes and types.

RADS
P.O. Box 5582
Wilmington, DE 19808
   Makes multi-colored grip tape that can stick onto your old grip tape.

National Skate
5408 South Proctor
Tacoma, WA 98409
(206) 473-3637
   Distributors of several national brands of skateboards and accessories.

Native Designs
1001-B Calle Negocio
San Clemente, CA 92672
(714) 361-0761

Rector Actionwear
Dressforit
P.O. Box 1654
Rohnert Park, CA 94928
(707) 584-4626
  Makes a full line of protective gear.

Rollermania
62 Park Row
Bristol BS15LE
United Kingdom
  Claims to be England's number one
skateboard shop.

Santa Cruz Skateboards
4401 Soquel Drive
Soquel, CA 95073
(408) 475-9434
  Makes Hosoi Skateboards and Speed
Wheels in a variety of densities and sizes.

Sessions
123 East Fremont Avenue
Sunnyvale, CA 94087
(408) 735-1137

SIO Barry
3447 Pheasant Court
Melbourne, FL 32935
  Offers Bionic hip padding, endorsed by
Tony Hawk. Also heel savers.

Sims Skateboards, Inc.
1711 Whittier Avenue
Costa Mesa, CA 92627
(714) 631-1800

Skate Core
P.O. Box 4957
Hayward, CA 95545
(415) 887-5819

Skate Rags
P.O. Box 84
Cardiff, CA 92007
(619) 721-9393

Skate Station
P.O. Box 115
Union City, CA 94587
(415) 887-4813

Skate Warehouse
141 D4 Suburban
San Luis Obispo, CA 93401

Skull Skates
15464 Cabrito Road
Van Nuys, CA 91408
(818) 994-4744

Slam Wrist Guards
835 West 24th Street
National City, CA 92050

Smoothill Sports Distributors
1595F Francisco
San Rafael, CA 94901

S.O.H. Skates on Haight
P.O. Box 170010
San Francisco, CA 94117-0010
(415) 431-5054
    A complete mail order house.

Steadham Designs
5519 Rawlings Street
Southgate, CA 90280
(213) 923-0724

Stick-Em Up
P.O. Box 769
Livermore, CA 94550

Stussy, Inc.
16631 Noyes
Irvine, CA 92714
(714) 474-9255

SuperCush Suspension
P.O. Box 8844234
San Francisco, CA 94188
    Makes soft, firm, and extra firm wheels.

TKE Enterprises
P.O. Box 6293
Santa Barbara, CA 93160

Thrasher Products
c/o Thrasher Magazine
P.O. Box 884570
San Francisco, CA 94188-4570
    Also carries skate rock cassettes, patches, ramp plans, banners, and more.

Tracker Trucks
Box 398
Cardiff, CA 92007
Makes Schmitt Stix curved rails.

Transworld Skateboarding
P.O. Box 3712
Escondido, CA 92025-9845
Also sells back issues of its magazine, art pencils, and banners.

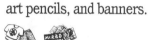

2DAC Video
1186 Yulupa Avenue
Santa Rosa, CA 95403
Carries videos featuring top amateurs.

Val Surf
P.O. Box 4576
North Hollywood, CA 91607
(818) 769-6977
A complete mail order house.

Venture Trucks
P.O. Box 883942
San Francisco, CA 94188-3982
Also offers instruction materials on skating.

Vision
1711 Whittier Avenue
Costa Mesa, CA 92627
Makes minis, complete skateboards, and Vision Street Wear.

Williamette Sports Center
2705 Williamette Street
Eugene, OR 97405
1 (800) 433-9601

Z Products
P.O. Box 5397
Santa Monica, CA 90405

Thunder Trucks
P.O. Box 884413
San Francisco, CA 94188

Tony Hawk / Team Stubbies
1900 Oakdale Avenue
San Francisco, CA 94124
Offers regular mailings to Hawk fans.

GLOSSARY

AGGRO. High or contorted, as in an "aggro air."

AIR. Any trick that gets a skater airborne while grabbing the board.

BACKSIDE HAND. In riding position, the hand that's closest to the nose of the board—also known as the lead hand.

BAIL. To fall off a board.

BIONIC. See Air.

BONED. A straight leg position used while riding or doing an invert. Same as "sad."

BONELESS. A trick done by pushing off the ground with one foot.

CARVE. To ride a curved line along a transition without your wheels leaving the ground. In vertical, carving is drifting through the air in an arc.

CASPER. A trick done standing on the rail of a board while kicking the deck in the direction you want to spin.

CHANNEL. A curved trough cut into the top of a ramp that lets you roll in.

COMPRESSING. Crouching or bending while riding to gain maximum speed and balance control.

COPING. The lip or rounded edge of a pool or ramp. Coping can be made of steel pipe, plastic pipe, or ceramic material.

CRAIL. A grab with your frontside hand on the nose.

DING. A bruise or wound from a skating accident.

EGGPLANT. An invert with an opposite grab; frontside hand on board, backside hand on coping.

FAKIE. Doing a trick or riding up a transition tail first.

50/50. In street and vertical skating, a 50/50 is any trick where you grind or slide on both axles or trucks.

FOOTPLANT. Any trick where you thrust off the top of the ramp with one foot.

FREESTYLE. A form of skateboarding and competition that puts the greatest value on doing many graceful, impressive tricks in a limited amount of time, usually to music.

FRONTSIDE HAND. In riding position, the hand closest to the tail of the board—also known as the trail hand.

GOOFY-FOOT. Riding or doing a trick with your right foot forward toward the nose of the board.

GRAB. Any of a variety of ways to hold the board while doing a trick.

GRAPHICS. Art that beautifies your board.

GRIND. Any trick where you ride up to a curb, lip, or coping and grind your axles on the edge.

HALF-PIPE. A skating ramp that forms an approximate semi-circle. A half-pipe usually is flat in the middle with a curved transition and vertical section at either end.

HANDPLANT. Any trick that calls for placing one hand on a surface and getting your body inverted. Same as invert.

INDY. A frontside grab on the frontside rail when you're turning backside.

INVERT. Any trick that calls for placing one hand on a surface and getting your body inverted. Same as handplant.

KICK-FLIP. A trick where you turn the board side-over-side in a complete flip and land back on the deck.

KICKTAIL. The angled tail of the board that is crucial to performing many tricks. It helps the skater pivot and compress and jump.

KICK-TURN. An abrupt turn made by kicking down on your kicktail, lifting up the nose, and planting it in another direction.

LIEN. A backside grab on the backside rail when you're turning frontside.

LIP. The edge of any riding surface, such as a pool or ramp.

MUTE. A grab with your backside hand on the frontside rail of the board.

NOSE. The front, forward-pointing end of a board.

NOSEPICK. Any trick where your front truck hits the coping, curb, or lip.

OLLIE. Any trick that gets a skater flying forward through the air without grabbing the board.

POGO. A balancing and hopping trick done on the upright tail.

POSEUR. A would-be skater who looks the part, but doesn't rip.

QUARTER-PIPE. A ramp that forms approximately one-fourth of a circle when viewed from the side. It allows skaters to get some air and do lip tricks.

RAD. Awesome, spectacular, sharp.

RAIL. Side of the board. Also a plastic or urethane accessory that runs lengthwise along the bottom edge of a skateboard to make sliding and grabbing easier.

RIP. Skate rad.

ROAD RASH. Knee or elbow burns from scraping the ramp or pavement.

SAD. A straight leg position used while riding or doing an invert. Same as boned.

SESSION. To have a good time skating a location.

SHRED. Skate rad.

SLIDE. Any maneuver where you slide out your tail, with your tail wheels skidding along as you change direction.

SNAKE. To cut off another skater.

SPACEWALK. Riding on the back wheels and moving the nose of the board left and right without letting the front wheels touch the ground.

STALL. Coming up to a lip, coping, or other edge and stopping briefly before dropping back in.

STOKED. Ready for action, excited.

STREET. A form of skating that grew out of doing tricks on streets, side-walks, curbs, and other common and uncommon obstacles. Also tricks done with street-type ramps such as launch and quarter-pipe.

TAIL. The back end of a board.

THRASHING. Skateboarding.

THRUSTER. A footplant done at the top of a ramp.

TIC-TAC. An old but popular move where you kick-turn left and right in rapid succession.

TRANSITION. An inclined riding surface of any kind, such as the curved or diagonal parts of ramps.

TRUCK. A mechanism that holds your axles, bearings, and wheels.

TWEAKED. A contorted trick position common to many inverts, usually with knee tucked and back arched.

VERTICAL. A form of skating that places greatest emphasis on tricks done on a half-pipe, including airs, inverts, and other moves.

WHEELIE. Any trick where you balance on one set of wheels, with the other end of the board in the air.

WILSON. A groin pull when one leg goes one direction and the other goes another direction.

ABOUT THE AUTHOR

Albert Cassorla, author of *The Skateboarder's Bible* in the 1970s, lives and skateboards with his family in suburban Philadelphia. He also writes plays and advertising copy.